Contents

STORYTIME PUPPET ZOO

Simple Puppet Patterns & Plays

Marilyn Lohnes

Published by **UpstartBooks**
W5527 Highway 106
P.O. Box 800
Fort Atkinson, Wisconsin 53538-0800
1-800-448-4887

© Marilyn Lohnes, 2005
Cover design: Debra Neu

The paper used in this publication meets the minimum requirements of American National Standard for Information Science — Permanence of Paper for Printed Library Material. ANSI/NISO Z39.48-1992.

Introduction

The childhood that I remember was full of imagination. We built forts, created nature crafts and played endless rounds of Red Rover and Duck, Duck, Goose. We invented new games and toys, and we entertained ourselves for hours on end.

How different it was from the childhood of today. Children in this generation are wrapped up in video games, satellite television and high speed computers. They rely heavily—but not entirely—on these items for their daily entertainment. Children of today are still as creative and inventive as their counterparts of a generation or two ago, but they struggle to identify themselves in some unique way.

Creativity abounds in puppetry. It encourages children to express themselves and to develop and expand their imagination. Watch the faces of children during a puppet presentation and you will know exactly what I mean. As the puppet, an inanimate object, is brought to life with their imagination, the children laugh and converse with the puppet and even warn it of impending danger.

Recently teachers and librarians have discovered the practical use of puppetry. Not only do puppets entertain—they educate. For the younger child they can foster language development. For the older child they can teach lessons and impart values; thus, they become an invaluable method of instruction and communication. Schools are becoming more interested in using puppetry as an entertaining and exciting way of teaching children and encouraging their creativity.

How To Use This Book

This book contains 25 simple animal puppet patterns that can be made by a teacher or librarian, or be prepared as a classroom project for children. You'll also find a list of picture books (organized by animal) that can be read as part of a curriculum theme and/or used to act out a puppet show.

Also included are five well-known animal puppet scripts that can be presented using the puppet patterns in the book. The plays are suitable for both preschool and school-age children. Classrooms may choose to present a puppet performance to a younger audience as part of a theater arts curriculum; or teachers or librarians may produce a more elaborate version of the show for a general or kindergarten audience. Patterns for a few simple props are included; other props might require some innovation and thought. With a little planning and preparation and a lot of imagination, children of all ages can be creatively inspired.

The Hand Puppet

The hand puppet is by far the most commonly used type of puppet. It is relatively simple to create and readily available to purchase for those who are not inclined to make their own. With a hand puppet, the puppeteer's hand is placed directly inside the puppet. Different fingers control the puppet's head and arms. These puppets can also pick up or manipulate props. The puppet becomes an extension of the puppeteer's own hand, making movements with the puppet seem more natural.

Holding a Hand Puppet

Although there are several ways to hold a hand puppet, a common method is to have the thumb and baby finger as the arms, and the index finger as the neck. The other two fingers are simply folded down. In this position the hand is more relaxed. The arms can spread the entire

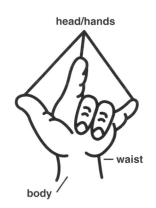

breadth of the body, and the wrist and neck joint are quick to manipulate. Some of the animal puppets, such as the turtle and fish, will pose a challenge. A fully spread hand probably works the best.

Movement of a Hand Puppet

There are three basic movements in hand puppetry. The first, done by moving the fingers, corresponds to puppet movements of the hands and head. The second, done by moving the wrist, corresponds to puppet movements of the waist. The third, done by moving the arm, corresponds to puppet movements as a whole unit, e.g., walking, running, jumping.

Maintaining Eye Contact

Eye contact gives the puppet the illusion of life. The audience will be looking where the puppets are looking, so be sure to plan the direction of the puppets. If one puppet is talking and the other puppet is looking at him, the puppets must face each other. Similarly, if the puppet is speaking to the audience, it must be looking at the audience. When looking at the audience, make sure the puppet is looking down, as the audience is generally seated on the floor.

Position of a Hand Puppet's Arms

Unless the puppeteer has remarkable flexibility in both the baby finger and the thumb, it is impossible for a hand puppet to hold its hands downward as though resting at the sides. For this reason, it is necessary to find another position that is both comfortable for the puppeteer and natural in appearance for the puppet. The arms may be held straight out in what is a comfortable position for the puppeteer. This appears a little awkward for a people puppet, however, it seems to make sense for an animal puppet. Another method is to rest the arms against the puppet's middle by folding both the thumb and the baby finger in. For animal puppets that are more personified this works well. The puppeteer can also manipulate props by simply reaching out and holding the prop with the thumb and baby finger.

Entering and Exiting the Stage

The entrance and exit of a puppet depends largely on its character. For a people puppet the basic entrance is tiered, meaning the puppet appears to come up a flight of stairs onto the stage. The exit is reversed, in that the puppet appears to descend a flight of stairs. Highly personified animal puppets can follow this basic entrance and exit routine. A snake, however, might slowly slither onstage, pause, then continue, while the rabbit might suddenly pop onstage, race across the opening and quickly depart. An elephant or a hippopotamus might heavily plod onto the stage, while a tiger or a cat might slink onstage from behind a curtain.

The typical walking movement of a puppet involves turning the puppet slightly from side to side while moving forward. For the hand puppet, this movement is done with the wrist to create waist movement in the puppet. Again, it may be necessary to adapt the walk for an animal puppet. A bird or an owl might hop from one spot to another, while a cow or an elephant might walk with a more pronounced sway. Always keep in mind the nature of the animal you are representing.

Basic Movements and Actions

A puppet is expected to act out his story, not only through speech, but also through actions. If the puppet is angry it might jump up and down. If it is unhappy it might slump over. The following is a list of some basic puppet actions and suggestions on how to accomplish the movement.

Crying: Arch the body backwards and, with jerking motions, bend the puppet at the waist.

Demonstrating Self: Draw the thumb or baby finger in to the puppet's middle to indicate pointing to self.

Excitement: Clap the hands by bringing the thumb and index finger together.

Nodding No: For hand puppets, the whole body must turn from side to side, as the head cannot do this on its own. Using the wrist, move the puppet slowly right, then left.

Nodding Yes: Wave the index finger slowly forward, then to an upright position.

Pointing: Raise one of the puppet's hands in the appropriate direction while holding the other against its body.

Snoring: Bend the waist of the puppet down, then with slow, jerking motions, raise it up.

Sneezing: Arch the body backwards, then as the sneeze lets go, bend the puppet at the waist.

Thinking: Rub the puppet head with one hand by moving either the thumb or the baby finger.

Animal Puppet Voices

Once you have practiced the basic movements and have given life to your puppet, you must decide what you want your puppet to sound like. Animal puppets need voices of their own, distinct from human voices so that the audience identifies with the puppet, not with the human who is manipulating the puppet.

Creating voices for puppets is really not all that difficult. We simply modify our human voices to become puppet voices. We begin with our own range of voice. We have a high-pitched voice, which we might use if excited, a natural speaking voice and a low or deep-throated voice, which might show disapproval or anger. Between these ranges are an infinite number of other voices, pitches and tones. Try experimenting with your voice by tape recording several samples of it in different ranges.

The next step in determining a puppet voice is matching the size of the puppet to the volume of the voice. A tiger puppet, for example, might have a loud, growling voice, whereas a mouse would have a small, soft, squeaking voice. This is important, as the audience must identify with each puppet separately. A tiger and a mouse who spoke similarly would be difficult to distinguish by the audience.

Once range and volume are established, the puppeteer must provide character to the voice. The job of the puppeteer is to convince the audience that the character he or she is presenting is real. There are a number of ways to accomplish this. One, as mentioned earlier, is to add a tone to the puppet's voice. The tiger's voice might be growly, while the mouse's voice might be squeaky. The cat's voice might be scratchy and high-pitched, while the turtle puppet might have a slow, sluggish voice. Another method is to use exaggerated alliteration. For example, a sheep puppet might exaggerate the letter "b" to make "baa." The speaking voice might be something like this: "Gee, that's too baaaaad, I'll have to go baaaack." Similarly, the cow might reply: "It's mmmoooost unfortunate, I hope you don't mmmmind."

Try imagining your puppet as a live character. Imagine what his voice would sound like, and then practice that sound using a tape recorder.

Creating Simple Puppet Stages

A puppet's world is the stage. Within it a puppet can run, play and generally behave as a human would. The opening of the stage, or proscenium, is the working area for the puppeteer and is generally seen by the audience as a picture frame in which the puppets perform. The puppets are easily seen, but the puppeteer is hidden from the audience behind the stage, either seated, kneeling or standing, depending on the stage. This creates a detachment between the puppet and the puppeteer, making the puppet characters seem more alive to the audience. The puppet's stage can be simple, yet very effective. Below are a few examples of simple puppet stages.

Doorway Stage

For the beginning puppeteer, a doorway stage is an easy way to create a puppet world. Simply stretch a blanket across an open doorway. The blanket should be at a height that is about two inches over the puppeteer's head when the puppeteer is seated or kneeling. The door frame creates a natural opening in which the puppeteer can perform.

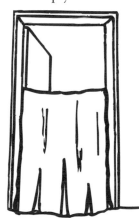

Table Stage

Another simple stage is the table stage. Turn a rectangular table on its side. Set the table in a suitable place for the puppet show, with the tabletop facing the audience. Drape blankets over the front and sides of the table. An option for a taller stage is to lay the table on top of another table that is standing upright.

Cardboard Box Stage

A cardboard box from a refrigerator can also make a nice, simple puppet stage. Remove the top and one side of the box, then stand the box on its bottom. Cut an opening for the stage with the bottom of the opening being approximately two inches above the puppeteer's head when he or she is sitting or kneeling.

Props, Backdrops & Lighting

With props and scenery it is easy to transform the stage into a forest, house, jungle or any place you want your puppets to be. The audience is transported into a time, place or mood with just a few props or a simple backdrop. The choice of props or scenery depends largely upon which type of stage you prefer to use, and how simple or professional you want your show to be.

Props

Props are objects other than the puppets that are used in a puppet presentation. Simple puppet stages generally don't lend themselves well to the use of heavy props, as these types of stages usually don't have a solid surface for placing prop items. Stick props would be the most suitable type of prop for simple stages. Two-dimensional props can be fastened to sticks and simply held up to the stage. Suspended props can also be used with simple stages. They can easily be manipulated by hanging some fishing line over a dowel, which is fastened to a door frame or a solid fixture above the stage. Props can effectively be raised or lowered using the suspended prop method.

Backdrops

Scenery is best presented through the use of backdrops. Backdrops are painted pieces of fabric that are hung behind the proscenium, or opening. A number of trees painted on a backdrop will indicate a forest to the audience, while a small house might suggest the puppet is on its way to that particular house. Scenes can be changed in two ways—they can be sewn or taped together and flipped over like a flip chart, or they can be placed on a rod with curtain rings, and one scene can simply be slid away while another one is introduced.

Lighting

Generally, as long as the room where the puppet show is being presented is well lit, no special lighting is required. However, some puppeteers prefer to have a light source in front of the stage shining directly onto the puppets. This can easily be done with a small floodlight or spotlight clamped to the outside of the puppet stage. Puppeteers may wish to experiment with colored lights. A green light would enhance a forest or jungle scene, while a blue light might suggest an underwater scene.

Sound & Special Effects

Music

Music enhances most puppet shows. It can be used to announce the beginning of a show, changes in scenes, particular moods or events and to announce the finale. Puppet shows with a particular theme require music related to that theme. For example, I open "The Monkey and the Crocodile" with calypso music. It is strongly advised to seek out the current copyright legislation regarding public performances of music. It may be necessary to purchase a background music license.

Taped Shows

As the puppeteer you must decide whether you will be performing live or taping the puppet show. A live show provides the performer with more control over the production and opportunities to interact with the audience. Taped shows are convenient in that all script, sound effects and music are incorporated into the recording. The puppeteer need do nothing more than press the "play" button and begin performing. Should you elect to tape your puppet show, be prepared to have several practice runs to match the script with the puppet's movements and speaking.

Special Effects

A puppet show is long remembered by its audience if a few special effects have been added. Here are a few simple suggestions to make your puppet show more exciting:

Sound Effects

- Fire: crumple a sheet of paper
- Galloping Animal: pat knees quickly
- Heavy Footsteps: turn a bucket upside down behind the stage and stomp on it
- Rain: whirl small marbles in a disposable aluminum pie plate
- Running Water: pour water from a mason jar into a larger jar or bucket
- Thunder: rattle disposable aluminum pie plates
- Tinkling Sounds: jingle car keys
- Wind: blow into an empty pop bottle

Special Effects

- Ice: saran wrap
- Icicles: icicle lights
- Lightning: turn light on and off
- Magic Wand: party sparkler
- Smoke: squeeze baby powder bottle
- Snow: white confetti

Turn a Fingerplay Into a Puppet Show

Preschool and kindergarten audiences love listening to fingerplays. They participate by holding up fingers and counting along with the presenter. Why not turn this opportunity into a puppet show? Five children can participate in each puppet show with five of the same puppet. The children can stand behind a stage or in a row, and can enter or exit depending on whether the rhyme is a count-up rhyme or a count-down rhyme. Some simple props can be added to incorporate other children in the show. Three or four different rhymes could mean that each child in the class has an opportunity to participate. Below are some suggestions of rhymes that could be converted into a puppet show.

Bats

Five Little Bats

Tune: "Five Bran Muffins" (Sidewalk Shuffle *by Sandra Beech. A & M Records, 1984.*)

Five little bats in a haunted house,
Five little bats, quiet as a mouse.
A witch came by with her cat one day,
The cat scared a bat and the bat flew away.
(Repeat for 4, 3, 2, 1.)

Bears

One Little Teddy Bear

One little teddy bear, crying "boo-hoo,"
Along came another, and then there were two.

Two little teddy bears, lonely as can be,
Along came another, and then there were three.

Three little teddy bears, looking for some more,
Along came another, and then there were four.

Four little teddy bears, one more to arrive,
Along came another, and then there were five.

Five little teddy bears had some fun today,
They'll be back again, and you can see them play.

Birds

One Little Bird

There was one little bird who lived up in a tree.
He was all alone, and he didn't want to be.
So he flew far away, over the big blue sea.
And he brought back a friend to live in the tree.
(Repeat for 2, 3, 4, 5.)

Cats

Five Little Kittens

Tune: "Faerie Song"

Five little kittens climbed up in a tree.
Five little kittens cried unhappily,
"Please help us down, this isn't very fun."
Along came Mr. Fireman, and down came one.
Along came Mr. Fireman, and down came one.
(Repeat for 4, 3, 2, 1.)

Chickens

Five Little Chickens

Tune: "Six Little Ducks"

Five little chickens, plump and round,
Pecked for seeds upon the ground.
One walked away from the farm that day,
When she found a little seed and carried it away.
(Repeat for 4, 3, 2, 1.)

Cows

Five Little Cows

Tune: "Camptown Races"

Five little cows ate grass all day,
Moo-moo, moo-moo.
Grazing in the fields of hay,
Moo-moo, moo-moo.
They ate and ate their fill.
They ate and ate until,
One little cow had enough that day,
And slowly walked away.
(Repeat for 4, 3, 2, 1.)

Crocodiles

One Crocodile

Tune: "If You're Happy and You Know It"

There was one crocodile on the Nile.
There was one crocodile on the Nile.
Oh, he looked for a while for another crocodile,
And he found a crocodile on the Nile.
(Repeat for 2, 3, 4, 5.)

Dogs

One Little Puppy

One little puppy with a rawhide chew,
Barked for a friend … *Woof!*
And then there were two.

Two little puppies, sniffing 'round a tree,
Barked for a friend … *Woof, Woof!*
And then there were three.

Three little puppies, no less, no more,
Barked for a friend … *Woof, Woof, Woof!*
And then there were four.

Four little puppies, wiggly and alive,
Barked for a friend … *Woof, Woof, Woof, Woof!*
And then there were five.

Five little puppies at the end of the day,
Heard their master calling …
And they all went away.

Ducks

Five Little Ducks

Traditional

Five little ducks went swimming one day
Over the hills and far away.
Mother duck said, "Quack, quack, quack."
But only four little ducks came back.
(Repeat for 4, 3, 2, 1.)

Sad Mother duck went swimming one day,
Over the hills and far away.
Mother duck said, "Quack, quack, quack."
And five little ducks came swimming back.

Elephants

One Large Elephant

Tune: "Row, Row, Row Your Boat"

One large elephant,
In the jungle sun,
Calls a friend around the bend,
And then along comes one.
(Repeat for 2, 3, 4.)

Fish

Five Little Fish

Tune: "Five Bran Muffins" (Sidewalk Shuffle *by Sandra Beech. A & M Records, 1984.)*

Five little fish in the farmer's pond,
Five little fish, swimming 'round and 'round.
A boy came fishing with his pole one day,
He caught a little fish and he carried it away.
(Repeat for 4, 3, 2, 1.)

No little fish in the farmer's pond,
No little fish, swimming 'round and 'round.
A boy came fishing with his pole one day,
Sorry little boy, no more fishing today.

Frogs

Five Green Frogs

Tune: "Frère Jacques"

Five green frogs, five green frogs,
On a log, on a log.
One jumps in the pool, where it's nice and cool.
Count with me, how many do you see?
(Repeat for 4, 3, 2, 1.)

Hippopotamuses

Five Hippopotamuses

Tune: "Row, Row, Row Your Boat"

Five hippopotamuses,
Wallow in the sun,
Thump and thud around the mud,
And then away goes one.
(Repeat for 4, 3, 2, 1.)

Mice

One Little Mouse

One little mouse, with a nibble and a chew,
Called for a friend … *Squeak!*
And then there were two.
Two little mice, quick as quick can be,
Called for a friend … *Squeak, Squeak!*
And then there were three.

Three little mice as they scampered 'round the floor,
Called for a friend … *Squeak, Squeak, Squeak!*
And then there were four.

Four little mice, with another to arrive,
Called for a friend … *Squeak, Squeak, Squeak, Squeak!*
And then there were five.

Monkeys

Five Little Monkeys Jumping on the Bed

Traditional

Five little monkeys jumping on the bed,
One fell off and bumped his head.
Momma called the doctor, and the doctor said,
"No more monkeys jumping on the bed!"
(Repeat for 4, 3, 2, 1.)

Owls

One Night Owl

Tune: "She'll be Coming 'Round the Mountain"

There was one night owl in the tree—*Who, Who.*
There was one night owl in the tree—*Who, Who.*
Oh, he called up to the sky to an owl flying by,
And the owl came and joined him happily—
Who, Who.
(Repeat for 2, 3, 4, 5.)

Pigs

Five Pink Piggies

Tune: "Five Brown Teddies" (Oranges and Lemons *by Karen King. Oxford, 1985.*)

Five pink piggies, wiggling in the mud.
Five pink piggies, wiggling in the mud.
If one pink piggy falls down with a "thud,"
There'd be four pink piggies, wiggling in the mud.
(Repeat for 4, 3, 2, 1.)

Rabbits

Fluffy Little Bunnies

Tune: "Jolly Old St. Nicholas"

Fluffy little bunnies,
1 … 2 … 3 … 4 … 5,
Waiting in their den for springtime to arrive.
Now it's a spring morning,
Out they come to play,
1 … 2 … 3 … 4 … 5
All on a spring day.

Raccoons

Five Little Raccoons

Tune: "Twinkle, Twinkle"

Five little raccoons by the lake,
Watch the antics that they make.
They splash the water, they climb a tree,
They climb the roofs of the houses—whee!
One little raccoon walks away,
How many raccoons stay to play?
(Repeat for 4, 3, 2, 1.)

Sheep

One Woolly Sheep

Tune: "One Elephant" (One Elephant, Deux Elephants *by Sharon, Lois & Bram. Elephant Records, 1986.*)

One woolly sheep with a woolly tail,
Frolicked through the meadow trail.
He had so much fun that day,
That he called for another sheep to come and play.
(Repeat for 2, 3, 4, 5.)

Skunks

Five Little Skunks

Tune: "Twinkle, Twinkle"

Five little skunks sitting in a row,
Black and white from head to toe.
They scuttled left, and they scuttled right,
One little skunk scuttled right out of sight.
How many skunks were left to see?
Count them carefully with me.
(Repeat for 4, 3, 2, 1.)

Snakes

One Snake

Tune: "She'll be Coming 'Round the Mountain"

There was one snake hiding in the grass—*Sss, sss.*
There was one snake hiding in the grass—*Sss, sss.*
Oh, he slithered 'round the bend where he met a new snake friend,
And the friend came and joined him at the pass—
Sss, sss.
(Repeat for 2, 3, 4, 5.)

Squirrels

Five Gray Squirrels

Tune: "Frère Jacques"

Five gray squirrels, five gray squirrels,
In a tree, in a tree.
One runs down the tree trunk,
One runs down the tree trunk,
And says he, "You can't catch me!"
(Repeat for 4, 3, 2, 1.)

Tigers

One Striped Tiger

Tune: "She'll be Coming 'Round the Mountain"

There was one striped tiger on the plain
  —*Grrr, grrr.*
There was one striped tiger on the plain
  —*Grrr, grrr.*
Oh he bounded 'round the bend,
Where he found a tiger friend,
And his jungle friend joined him on the plain
  —*Grrr, grrr.*

Turtles

One Little Turtle

One little turtle on the pond so blue,
Called for a friend, and then there were two.

Two little turtles snapped at a bee,
One came for lunch, and then there were three.

Three little turtles on a log near the shore,
One crawled up with them, and then there were four.

Four little turtles, ready now to dive,
One swam up to them, and then there were five.

Five little turtles dove into the pond,
As they waved to their friends, "Good-bye, so long!"

The Little Red Hen

(On the Farm)

Number of Puppets: 4	**Props:**
• Little Red Hen (p. 70)	• wheat (p. 22)
• Cow (p. 70)	• pail (p. 22)
• Sheep (p. 77)	• cake (p. 22)
• Duck (p. 72)	
Playing Time: 15–20 minutes	**Music:** country

Scene 1

Action: *Outside farm. Hen is onstage.*

Hen: Thank goodness I got away from that smelly old farm. Farmer Brown never cleaned the animals' stalls and I always had to do it. And those animals! What slobs they were. They never even tried to keep their places tidy. I'm so glad I ran away and found this abandoned farm. It needs a little work, but it will be spiffy in no time.

Cow: *(Arriving onstage.)* Good to see you again, Miss Hen.

Hen: *(Annoyed.)* Oh, it's you.

Cow: Nnnnice place. *(Looking around.)* Is it yours?

Hen: Of course it's mine.

Cow: It's clean.

Hen: Of course it's clean. It's mine.

Cow: It's perfect.

Hen: Perfect? Perfect for what?

Cow: Why, perfect for moooving in!

Hen: Moving in? You're not moving in. This is my place!

Cow: *(Pushes past Hen.)* Yes, I think this will be mmmooost comfortable. *(Exits.)*

Hen: *(Annoyed.)* This isn't a boarding house, you know …

Sheep:	*(Arriving onstage.)* Hello, Miss Hen.
Hen:	*(Moaning.)* Not you, too …
Sheep:	Nnnnice place you have here.
Hen:	Yes, and it's mine! Just for me.
Sheep:	You know, I've bbbeen looking for a clean place to stay. My bbbed bbaaack home is pretty bbbaaad since you left.
Hen:	Well you can't move in here.
Cow:	*(Offstage.)* Hey sheep, come on in and see this place. It's mmmagnificent!
Hen:	*(To sheep.)* Oh no you don't!
Sheep:	*(Pushing through.)* Oh, I bbbet it's bbbeautiful! *(Exits.)*
Hen:	*(Angry.)* Oh, this is infuriating!
Duck:	*(Arriving onstage.)* Hello, Miss Hen. Glad to see you're doing alright.
Hen:	I was doing just finc until you guys showed up.
Duck:	You mean there are others here?
Hen:	*(Annoyed.)* Yes, Cow and Sheep showed up a few minutes ago, and I've been trying …
Duck:	Cow and Sheep are here? Oooooh, that's ducky!
Hen:	Don't you think for a minute that …
Duck:	*(Pushes past Hen.)* Ooohh, this is great! We're all together again! *(Exits.)*
Hen:	I can't believe it. I left the farm to get rid of these slobs, and now I have the three of them in my new, clean farm. *(Exits.)*

Scene 2

Action:	*Hen is onstage alone.*
Hen:	*(Angrily.)* Oooh, I can't believe it! I left these creatures to have some peace and quiet … and a clean place to stay. Now the barn is just as dirty as before, and I'm cooking for all three of them.
Sheep:	*(Enters.)* I'm starving! What's for supper?
Hen:	Corn casserole.
Sheep:	Corn again? That's bbbaaad, Miss Hen, we've had corn three times a day.

Cow:	*(Enters.)* Three times a day for the past three weeks. That's toooo mmmmuch.
Duck:	Yeah. That's not even a good diet for a duck.
Hen:	Well, I spend all of my day cleaning up after you three. If you would just put a little work into it yourselves, I might have time to go into town and buy something else.
Duck:	I'm not cleaning up after Cow. She's really messy!
Cow:	Mmmme? I'm not the mmmmessy one. It's Sheep!
Sheep:	Nnnno way. It's Duck who leaves baaaaad messes everywhere!
Action:	*Animals begin to argue.*
Hen:	Never mind. I'll clean everything up myself. You three can stay here and eat corn. I'm going for a walk! *(Exits.)*
Duck:	*(Calling after Hen.)* What about us? *(Exits.)*
Sheep:	Are you coming baaaack soon? *(Exits.)*
Cow:	We want sommmmething else to eat! *(Exits.)*

Scene 3

Action:	*Hen enters quickly onstage.*
Hen:	*(Running.)* Come quickly! Look what I found!
Sheep:	*(Enters, runs into Hen.)* You're baaack! What did you bbring us?
Hen:	I have a grain of wheat!
Sheep:	A grain of wheat? You came baaack and all you brought was a grain of wheat? I don't want a grain of wheat!
Hen:	Well that's good, because I wasn't offering it to you. I want you to help me plant it.
Sheep:	I can't. I've got a baaad baaack. *(Exits.)*
Hen:	Some excuse! Oh, here comes Cow.
Cow:	*(Enters.)* Mmmmiss Hen, you're back!
Hen:	Yes, and look what I have! A grain of wheat.
Cow:	Not mmmuch of a mmmmeal, but I'll take it. *(Tries to eat grain.)*
Hen:	It's not for eating, you silly cow, it's for planting! Come help me plant it.

Cow:	Nothin' doing. You mmmade fun of me! Calling mmme a silly cow. I'mmmm leaving! *(Exits.)*
Hen:	Oh dear, they're all so sensitive. I'll just have to ask Duck. Here he comes now.
Duck:	*(Enters.)* Hello there, Miss Hen. Nice of you to come back. I thought your feathers were a little ruffled earlier.
Hen:	Well, yes, but look what I have now—a grain of wheat.
Duck:	Don't get your tail feathers in a knot. Just throw it in the grass and nobody will notice it.
Hen:	Throw it away? I don't want to throw it away. I want you to help me plant it.
Duck:	Plant it? What for? I have better things to do with my time! *(Exits.)*
Hen:	*(Yelling after Duck.)* Like maybe cleaning up your living quarters? Oooh, they make me so mad! I suppose I'll have to plant the grain of wheat myself. *(Plants seed and exits.)*

Scene 4

Action:	*Hen enters with pail.*
Hen:	Oh, my goodness, what warm weather we've been having. My wheat needs watering quite badly. I've just filled this pail with water and I'll see if I can get someone to help me carry it to the wheat. Oh, here comes Duck. I'll ask him.
Duck:	*(Enters.)* Hey there, Miss Hen. What's in the pail?
Hen:	I have some water. I was hoping that you could help me water …
Duck:	*(Interrupting.)* Water! What a ducky idea. A nice hot day like today is perfect for a swim! *(Jumps into pail.)*
Hen:	Oh, stop it! Stop it! You're spilling all the water!
Duck:	You know, Miss Hen, if you're going to have a swimming pool it should be bigger. *(Exits.)*
Hen:	I can't believe what that duck just did! There's hardly any water left in the pail. I'll have to go back and … oh, here comes Cow. I'll ask her for some help.
Cow:	*(Enters.)* What mmmight you have there, Mmmiss Hen?
Hen:	I have some water for watering the wheat. It's not much, you see, because Duck went and …
Cow:	*(Interrupting.)* Water, you say! That would be mmmoost appreciated. *(Leans into pail and drinks.)*

Hen:	Oh my goodness! Stop it! You're drinking all the water!
Cow:	*(Making slurping noises.)* Mmmm. That hit the spot. *(Exits.)*
Hen:	Honestly, I can't believe those two. They didn't leave me a drop of water. Maybe Sheep will help me. I see him coming. *(Calling.)* Oh, Sheep!
Sheep:	*(Enters.)* You bleated?
Hen:	No. I called for your help. I have this pail for watering the wheat. It was full, but between Cow and Duck …
Sheep:	Miss Hen, I don't mean to be so rude, but there's no water in the pail.
Hen:	Yes, I know. I was hoping you would help me fetch some water and carry it out to water the …
Sheep:	Can't. You know, that baaad baaack of mine … *(Exits.)*
Hen:	These three aren't much help at all. They eat all of my corn, they leave their rooms a mess, and they refuse to help me when I ask. I guess I'll have to water the wheat myself. *(Exits with pail.)*

Scene 5

Action:	*Hen enters, looking at wheat.*
Hen:	Oh, my wheat is wonderfully ripe. Now's the time to cut it and take it to the mill to be ground. I can cut it myself *(makes cutting actions)*, but I will need help getting it to the miller. Maybe Cow will help. Here she comes now. *(Calling.)* Oh, Cow!
Cow:	*(Enters.)* You mooed for mmme?
Hen:	In a manner of speaking, yes. Can you help me carry this wheat to the mill to be ground into flour?
Cow:	Carry? What do you take me for, a common farm animal?
Hen:	You are a common farm animal.
Cow:	That, Mmmiss Hen, was mmoost impolite! *(Exits.)*
Hen:	*(Yelling as Cow leaves.)* Well don't have a **cow!** Good grief, whatever next! Oh, here comes Duck.
Duck:	*(Enters.)* Nnnaa, what's up duck? *(Giggles.)* I always wanted to say that!
Hen:	Yes, well, I was hoping you could help me carry this wheat to the mill to be made into flour.

Duck:	You don't need any more flowers, Miss Hen. There are flowers all over the place. See, there's some yellow flowers over there, and there's some white ones. There's plenty of flowers. *(Exits.)*
Hen:	*(Calling after Duck.)* No, I meant flour. The kind that you make bread from. Oh, good grief!
Sheep:	*(Entering.)* What's wrong? Something baaad happen?
Hen:	Oh, Sheep. I've been trying to get someone to help me carry this wheat to the mill to be made into flour.
Sheep:	Don't look at me. I've got a baaad …
Hen:	Back. Yes I know. *(Sheep exits.)* I guess I'll have to drag the wheat myself. *(Drags wheat and exits.)*

Scene 6

Action:	*Hen is in the kitchen baking a cake.*
Cow:	*(Enters.)* What is that smell? It's simply mmmarvelous.
Sheep:	*(Enters.)* Doesn't smell half baaaad, does it?
Duck:	*(Enters.)* Mmm. Did you bake quackers?
Hen:	I made a cake from my wheat.
Cow:	Mmmmay I help you eat it?
Duck:	I'll help you out with the crumbs.
Sheep:	I'll have some cake too, and I'll take some baaatter if there's any left.
Hen:	Oh, ho! So now you want to help out! None of you would help me plant the wheat. None of you would help me water it. Not one of you helped me carry it to the mill or bake it. And now you want to eat it?
Duck, Sheep and Cow:	*(Looking at each other.)* YES!
Hen:	You lazy, smelly slobs! I've put up with you long enough. Out of my home! Out! *(Flaps wings and clucks loudly, chasing animals offstage.)* Go back to Farmer Brown!
	Finally, peace and quiet. I'll start cleaning my place tomorrow. Today I'm going to enjoy a delicious warm cake.

Cake–Photocopy, color, cut out and mount on stick.
Pail–Photocopy, color, cut out and mount on stick.
Wheat–Photocopy, color, cut out and mount on stick.

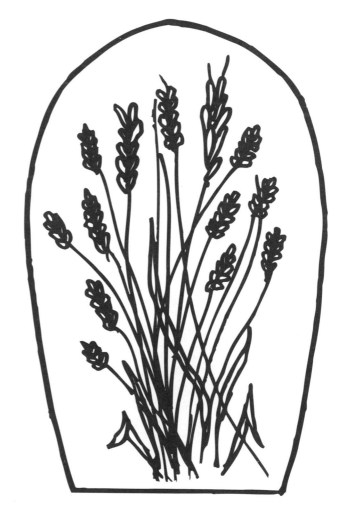

The Monkey and the Crocodile

Number of Puppets: 5	**Props:**
• Monkey (p. 74)	• palm trees (p. 28)
• Second Monkey (appearance only) (p. 74)	• banana trees (p. 27)
• Third Monkey (appearance only) (p. 74)	• large rock (p. 28)
• Crocodile 1 (p. 71)	**Music:** calypso
• Crocodile 2 (p. 71)	**Sound Effects:** group of monkeys chattering
Playing Time: 10–15 minutes	

Scene 1

Action: *A large group of monkeys are chattering in the trees, eating fruit. Two crocodiles are below, watching.*

Crocodile 1: Man, I'm hungry, what I wouldn't give for a tasty monkey right about now.

Crocodile 2: Sounds good, but I don't see how you're going to catch a monkey. They're pretty fast. Look. *(Points to trees.)* Look at that one move!

Crocodile 1: Yeah. He sure moves fast, even faster than his friends. Yep, that's the one I want.

Crocodile 2: He's faster than you are.

Crocodile 1: Yeah, but I'm smarter.

Crocodile 2: Well Einstein, there's another problem.

Crocodile 1: Yeah, what's that?

Crocodile 2: *(Pointing.)* They live on the land, and we live in the water.

Crocodile 1: Hmmm, I'll think of something. There must be a way for a crocodile to catch a monkey. I'll sleep on it tonight. *(Crocodiles exit.)*

Scene 2

Action:	*Monkey and Crocodile are onstage together.*
Crocodile 1:	*(To monkey.)* Hey, Monkey, how would you like to go over to that island over there for some delicious bananas?
Monkey:	Why would I need to go over there? There are plenty of bananas over here.
Crocodile 1:	But those bananas are much sweeter.
Monkey:	Really? I thought they all tasted the same.
Crocodile 1:	Oh, no. The bananas on that island are better than any others.
Monkey:	*(Looking out to the water.)* But I don't know how to swim.
Crocodile 1:	That's alright. I can carry you over on my back.
Monkey:	Oooh, that sounds wonderful. *(Calls to friends.)* Hey, Gabby, Doodles, wanna come for a ride? *(Two monkeys arrive onstage, shriek with fright and exit.)* Gee. I wonder what's wrong with them?
Crocodile 1:	Yes, well never mind. Come on, Monkey, climb aboard.
Monkey:	*(Climbs on Crocodile's back.)* Ooohhh, isn't this fun!
Crocodile 1:	Oh, you're going to have fun, alright. *(Swims away from shore.)*
Monkey:	Hey, isn't the island that way?
Crocodile 1:	Oh, I have to swim in the deep water. We'll go around the island and land on the other side.
Monkey:	*(Hesitating.)* Oh.
Crocodile 1:	Hey, Monkey, what do you think of this? *(Dives down underwater, comes up to surface.)*
Monkey:	*(Spitting and coughing.)* What did you do that for?
Crocodile 1:	Did you like it? Let's try it again! *(Dives under and up again.)*
Monkey:	*(Coughing.)* Oh, please, don't do that any more. I don't like it.
Crocodile 1:	Don't like it, huh? Well what would you say if I told you I was going to do it again? Only **this** time I'm going to go underwater for a long, long time. You're going to drown, and then I'm going eat you up!
Monkey:	No, please don't do that! Please, please!
Crocodile 1:	Why shouldn't I?
Monkey:	*(Thinking fast.)* Because … because if you ate me now you wouldn't get to taste my heart. I don't have it with me.

Crocodile 1:	Your heart? What do I need your heart for?
Monkey:	Didn't you know? The heart is the tastiest part of a monkey.
Crocodile 1:	Really? I didn't know that.
Monkey:	Oh, yes, it's really the best part of us. But unfortunately I left it hanging on the tree when we left.
Crocodile 1:	*(Greedily.)* Well, then we'll just have to go back for it.
Monkey:	We're awfully near the island. Couldn't we go there first?
Crocodile 1:	No sir! We're going straight back to get your heart. *(Swims quickly.)* Here we are, at the bank.
Monkey:	*(Jumps off Crocodile's back and into tree.)* My heart is way up here in the tree. If you want it, come and get it! *(Laughs.)*
Crocodile 1:	This isn't the end, Monkey. I'll get you yet!
	(Crocodile swims offstage, Monkey jumps offstage.)

Scene 3

Action:	*Monkey is onstage. Tree is to side of stage, rock is in middle of stage.*
Monkey:	I'm so glad I moved farther down the river. My friends aren't around, but neither is that mean old Crocodile. And now, I can hop over to the island and back on that rock in the middle of the river. *(Hops onto rock and back, then exits.)*
Crocodile 1:	*(Enters talking to audience.)* So, **this** is where that monkey went. He thinks he's so smart going across to the island on that rock. I bet he'll be over on that island all day. But I know how to catch him on his way back tonight. I'll just climb onto the rock and I'll wait for him. Tonight he'll be my supper! *(Climbs onto rock.)*
Monkey:	*(Enters onstage.)* Mmm. Those bananas really are delicious. I'm so full. I guess it's time to head back to the river bank. *(Looks at rock.)* Hmm. Something's wrong with that rock. It's never been that high before. I think someone is lying on it. *(Loudly.)* Hello, rock. *(No answer.)* Hello, rock. *(No answer.)* Mr. Rock, why won't you answer me tonight?
Crocodile 1:	*(To audience.)* Oh, the rock must talk to the monkey at night. I'll have to answer for the rock. *(To monkey.)* Yes my friend Monkey, what is it?
Monkey:	*(Laughing.)* Oh, it's you, Crocodile.

Crocodile 1:	It's me, alright. I've been waiting for you here, and now I'm going to eat you up!
Monkey:	I see. You certainly have caught me **this** time. I have no other way to get home. *(Thinking.)* Maybe, Mr. Crocodile, you could open your mouth wide so that I can jump inside. *(To audience.)* I know that when the crocodile opens his mouth he will close his eyes.
Crocodile 1:	Okay, Monkey, I'm opening my mouth. *(Opens mouth wide, Monkey jumps onto Crocodile's head and then onto river bank.)*
Monkey:	Beat you again, Mr. Crocodile!
Crocodile 1:	So you did, Monkey. I thought I was clever, but I see that you are even more clever. I'll leave you alone from now on.
Monkey:	Thank you … but I think I'll keep my eye open for you. On second thought, I think I'll keep both eyes open! *(Both exit.)*

Banana Tree–Photocopy, color, cut out and mount on stick.

Palm Tree–Photocopy, color, cut out and mount on stick.

Rock–Photocopy, color, cut out and mount on stick.

The Three Little Pigs

<table>
<tr><td>

Number of Puppets: 6
- Mother Pig (p. 75)
- First Little Pig (p. 75)
- Second Little Pig (p. 75)
- Third Little Pig (p. 75)
- Wolf (**Note:** for Wolf, use dog puppet on page 71, making pointed ears and teeth.)
- Bear (p. 68)

Playing Time: 10–15 minutes

</td><td>

Props:
- house of straw (p. 34)
- house of sticks (p. 35)
- house of bricks (p. 36)
- small pile of straw (p. 33)
- small pile of sticks (p. 33)
- small pile of bricks (p. 33)
- pot (p. 37)

Music: Most of the music in this puppet show is provided by singing. If the presenter wants extra music, classical works well.

</td></tr>
</table>

Scene 1

Action:	*Three little pigs playing ring-around-the-rosy. Chant song. Enter Mother Pig, crying.*
Mother:	Oh … There you are, my little sausages. *(Cries.)*
First Pig:	What's the matter, Mother?
Second Pig:	Why are you crying?
Mother:	Oh! Boo hoo, I have some sad news.
Third Pig:	What is it, Mother? Please tell us.
Mother:	Oh, times are bad—we've used up all our money.
First Pig:	Even the money from our piggy banks?
Mother:	Yes, even the money from our piggy banks. Oh, boo hoo.
Second Pig:	What are we going to do?
Mother:	I must send you out to seek your fortunes!
First Pig:	Oh boy, we're off to seek our fortunes!
Second Pig:	Off to have a good time.
Third Pig:	Off to stand on our own two hooves!
Mother:	Good-bye, my little pork chops. *(Kisses each one loudly.)* I've always protected you, but now that you will be on your own, I cannot. I have one last warning, my sweet little sausages: beware of the big bad Wolf.

All Pigs:	Yes, Mother, we know, we'll be careful. *(Pigs exit.)*
Wolf:	*(Entering.)* Did I just see three little piggies go by? Yummmeee. Pork pie, crispy bacon, grilled ham. *(Exits.)*
First and Second Pig:	*(Enter dancing and singing.)* Who's afraid of the big bad wolf …
Third Pig:	You two should be afraid of the wolf. After all, he does eat pigs.
Second Pig:	Don't be such a worrywart, brother.
First Pig:	Yeah, we can look after ourselves.
Third Pig:	Suit yourselves, but I'm going to build a good strong house. Mother warned us about the wolf, and I'm going to listen.

Scene 2

Action:	*Enter First Little Pig.*
First Pig:	Sizzling sausages! I'm supposed to build a house. But what am I going to use to build a house? I'd rather play than build a house, so I want to use something that won't take all day to make. Now, let's see …
Bear:	*(Enters, carrying straw and singing the tune "A Hunting We Will Go.")* It's off to market I go with a load of straw, Ho! Ho! It's yellow like gold and hard to hold this pile of straw of mine.
First Pig:	Straw! **That's** it! Please Mr. Bear, may I have some of that straw to build me a house?
Bear:	You may have it if you like, but it won't make a very strong house.
First Pig:	Thank you, Mr. Bear. *(Takes straw, Bear exits.)* Who needs a strong house anyway? There, now I'll just put up a little straw here and a little straw there *(put up house)* and a window. There! All done. Doesn't it look sturdy? *(Pig leans on house and it almost tips over.)* Now I'll just go inside and rest for a bit.
Wolf:	*(Enters sniffing.)* Mmm. I smell something good. Boys and girls, is it chicken I smell? No—rabbit? No—pig?
Wolf:	Yes, it's pig. *(Knocks on door.)* Little pig, little pig, let me come in.
First Pig:	Oooohhh, not by the hair on my chinny chin chin.
Wolf:	Then I'll **huff** and I'll **puff** and I'll **blow** your house in. *(Wolf does so, Pig squeals after each blow, house caves in after third blow.)*
First Pig:	Oh, no! My house, where's my house, where's my mommy! *(Pig runs.)*
Wolf:	Stop, my little pork hock, I'll get you yet. *(Pig escapes.)* Rats, he got away. *(Wolf exits.)*

Scene 3

Action: *Enter Second Little Pig.*

Second Pig: I suppose I should at least **try** to build a house of some sort. After all, mother **did** say to build something. Now, what can I use to build a house?

Bear: *(Enters, carrying sticks and singing to the tune "A Hunting We Will Go.")* I'm off to town today. To sell my load of sticks. There's long ones and there's short ones too, exactly the right mix.

Second Pig: Sticks! That sounds good enough for me. Please Mr. Bear, may I have some of those sticks to build me a fine home?

Bear: Well, of **course** you can have some. I was just cleaning out my shed and I don't need them any more. But are you sure you want to build your house of sticks?

Second Pig: They'll do just fine, Mr. Bear. *(Takes sticks.)* Thank you very much. *(Exit Bear.)* This will be strong enough. There, now I'll just put a few sticks here and there and *(puts up house)* I'll put a window here. What do you think, boys and girls? *(Taps on house and it nearly falls over.)*

Wolf: *(Enters sniffing.)* Ahhh, maybe this is my lucky day after all. *(Sniffs more around house.)* Yessir, I see pork and beans for supper. *(Knocks on door.)* Little pig, little pig, let me come in.

Second Pig: Ooooohhh, not by the hair on my chinny chin chin.

Wolf: Then I'll **huff** and I'll **puff** and I'll **blow** your house in. *(Wolf does so, Pig squeals after every blow, house caves in after third blow.)*

Second Pig: Oooooohhh, I don't **want** to be bacon, I don't **want** to be bacon.

Wolf: Slow down pig, I like my pork chops tender. *(Pig escapes.)* **Rats,** he got away. Those little porkers can sure run fast. *(Wolf exits.)*

Scene 4

Action: *Enter Third Little Pig.*

Third Pig: Gee, I wonder how my brothers are getting along. I hope they **listened** and built themselves safe homes. Now I'm going to start my home. I need something very strong to build my home with. Now, what should I use?

Bear: *(Enters, carrying bricks and singing to the tune "A Hunting We Will Go.")* I'm off to market once more, just like I was before. This time with bricks, a heavy mix to carry all the way.

Third Pig:	Bricks! Now they would be a fine thing to build a house from. Please Mr. Bear, may I have those fine bricks of yours?
Bear:	What would you like them for, little pig?
Third Pig:	*(Singing.)* I'll use these fine bricks, To build me a home, 'Cause I promised my mother, That I'd never roam. There's a big bad wolf, Who'll eat me up fast, Unless I build a house, That will last and last and last.
Bear:	For such a worthy cause, you are **welcome** to my bricks. Good luck. *(Bear exits.)*
Third Pig:	Thank you Mr. Bear, and good-bye. Boy, bricks are sure heavy, but a good strong house is **worth** all the hard work. Now I'll just put up one wall at a time *(puts up house)* and I'll have a fine chimney. *(Puts up chimney.)* There, I've got a wolf-proof house. Now I'll just go inside and finish up the fireplace.
Wolf:	*(Enters sniffing.)* I smell a pork roast for supper and **this** time I'm not going to let it get away. *(Knocks on door.)* Little pig, little pig, let me come in.
Third Pig:	No sir, not by the hair on my chinny chin chin.
Wolf:	Then I'll **huff** and I'll **puff** and I'll **blow** your house in.
Third Pig:	Go ahead and try, Mr. Wolf. This house is solid brick, you'll blow your **teeth** out before you blow **my** house down.
Wolf:	Not so fast, my handsome ham. I haven't tried yet. *(Wolf blows at house but nothing happens, tries again, nothing.)*
Third Pig:	*(Giggles and sings.)* Who's afraid of …
Wolf:	Well, I'm not finished yet. Boys and girls, what do you think I should do? The chimney, you say? I'll just climb down the chimney. *(Slowly starts to climb up side of house.)*
Third Pig:	Uh, oh. I'd better do something about that wolf. *(Sneaks outside, grabs pot of water.)* I'll just put this pot of water over the fireplace and that wolf will slide down right into boiling water. *(Wolf slides down chimney. A loud roar and splash is heard.)*
Third Pig:	Now when my little brothers come to visit, I can serve them **wolf** stew. *(Exits singing.)* Who's afraid …

Small Pile of Straw–Photocopy, color, cut out and mount on stick.

Small Pile of Sticks–Photocopy, color, cut out and mount on stick.

Small Pile of Bricks–Photocopy, color, cut out and mount on stick.

House of Straw–Enlarge to desired size. Photocopy, color, cut out and mount on cardboard.

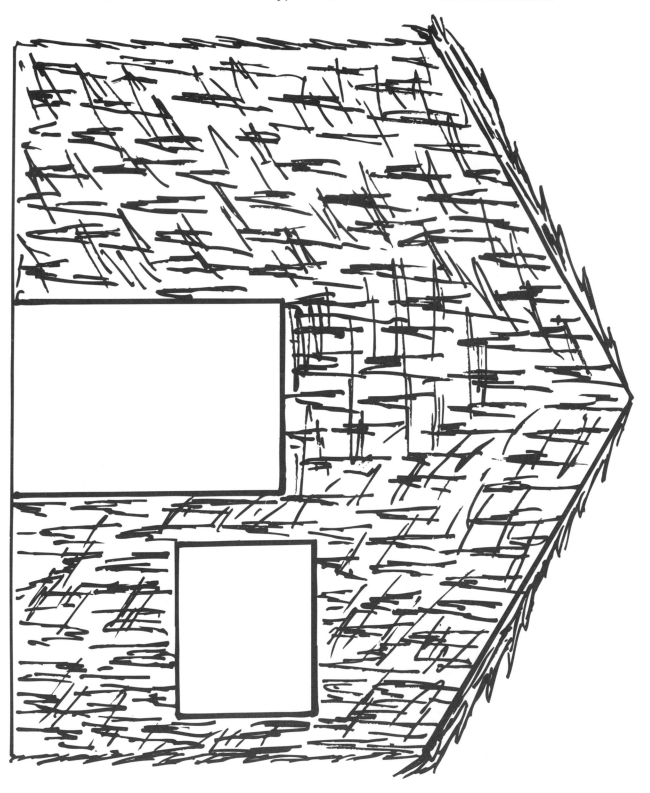

House of Sticks–Enlarge to desired size. Photocopy, color, cut out and mount on cardboard.

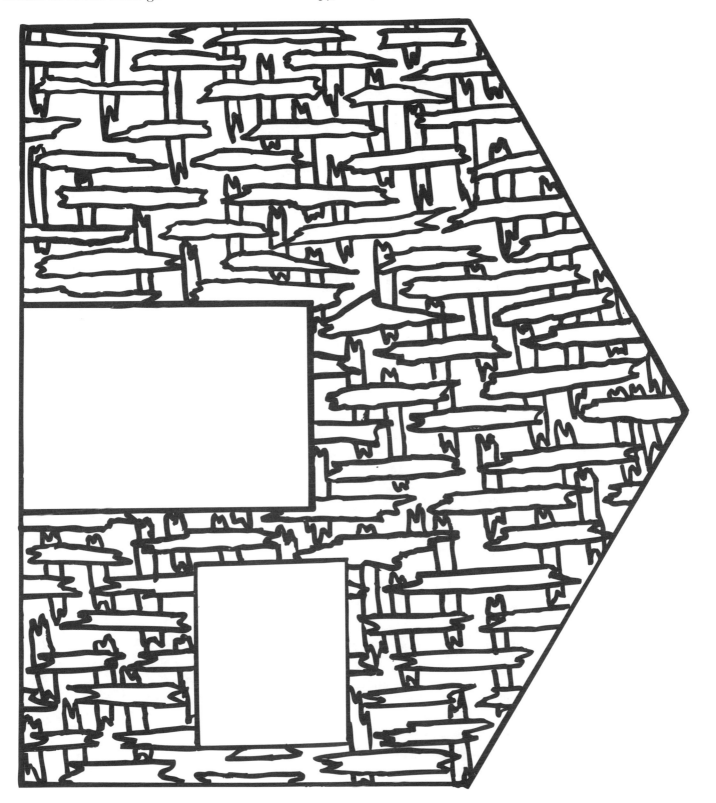

House of Bricks–Enlarge to desired size. Photocopy, color, cut out and mount on cardboard.

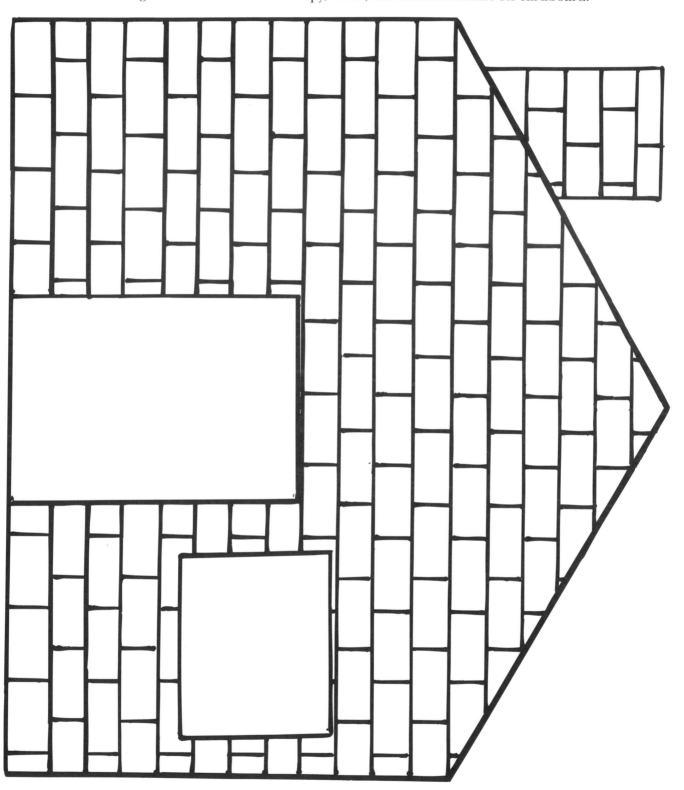

Pot–Photocopy, color, cut out and mount on a stick.

The Tortoise and the Hare

Number of Puppets: 5	**Props:**
• Sammy Squirrel (p. 78)	• concession stand (p. 43)
• Stephen Skunk (p. 77)	• cup of water (p. 45)
• Harry Hare (p. 76)	• can of soda pop (p. 45)
• Tommy Tortoise (p. 79)	• pizza (p. 46)
• Ricky Raccoon (delivery person) (p. 76)	• lettuce (p. 45)
Playing Time: 15–20 minutes	**Music:** Any fast-paced music.

Scene 1

Action:	*Stephen Skunk and Sammy Squirrel onstage.*
Squirrel:	Nice day, isn't it, Stephen?
Skunk:	It sure is. Hey! Maybe we can go on a picnic together?
Squirrel:	That sounds great. I have some peanut butter at home, and …
Action:	*Harry Hare enters on other side of stage.*
Skunk:	*(Interrupting.)* Shhh. It's Harry Hare.
Squirrel:	Where?
Skunk:	*(Pointing.)* Over there. He's always making fun of me.
Squirrel:	Yeah, me too.
Skunk:	*(Sighing.)* He calls me "Stinky Face."
Squirrel:	He calls me "Fluff-n-puff."
Hare:	*(Calling over.)* Hey, Stinky Face, Fluff-n-puff …
Action:	*Sammy Squirrel and Stephen Skunk mutter under their breath.*
Hare:	Whatcha' doin'?
Squirrel:	*(Hesitating.)* Nothing …
Skunk:	Nothing!
Hare:	Oh. *(Turns to Squirrel and chuckles.)* Because I thought you might be giving ol' Stinky Face a bath! Ha, ha, ha! … or … wait … *(turns to Skunk and chuckles)* maybe you're both going to take baths, and you're going to dry your friend on the fluff cycle! Ha! Ha, ha! Oh, I'm **good.**

38

Squirrel:	*(Mumbling.)* You may be good, but you're not very nice.
Hare:	So what? What does nice get you anyway?
Skunk:	Nice gets you friends, Harry, and friends are important.
Hare:	Says who? I don't need any friends, I'm better than everyone else.
Squirrel:	You can't say that, Harry. Nobody is a better person than someone else.
Action:	*Tommy Tortoise enters stage.*
Hare:	Well, I'm better. I'm better at everything. Why, I can even … *(Trips over Tommy Tortoise. Sammy Squirrel and Stephen Skunk laugh loudly.)*
Skunk:	*(Laughing.)* Doesn't look like you're much good at walking, Harry!
Squirrel:	*(Roaring with laughter.)* Yeah, Harry, but you're the best at tripping!
Hare:	That's not funny! *(Turns to Tommy Tortoise.)* Why don't you watch where you're going, slowpoke?
Tortoise:	Why don't you watch where you're going?
Squirrel:	*(Laughing.)* Good one, Tommy!
Hare:	*(Annoyed.)* Oh, so you think that's funny? I'll tell you what would be funny … me challenging ol' slowpoke here to a race. That's enough to make **anyone** laugh. So, what do you think, slowpoke, up to the challenge? Tomorrow morning?
Tortoise:	Sure I am!
Skunk:	You know, Tommy, you don't have to do this.
Squirrel:	Yeah, Tommy, he's just trying to upset you.
Hare:	You two stay out of this. This is between Tommy and me.
Tortoise:	It's okay guys, Harry and I can have a race.
Hare:	*(Laughing.)* Yeah, we can have a race, but I'll win, even with my eyes closed.
Tortoise:	You wouldn't want to close your eyes, Harry. You might trip over me again!
Action:	*Stephen Skunk and Sammy Squirrel laugh loudly.*
Hare:	Let's see who's laughing tomorrow when I win the race. *(Exits.)*
Skunk:	You know it's not too late to change your mind, Tommy.
Tortoise:	Don't worry about me. Besides, I think it would do Harry some good to lose a race.
Squirrel:	Lose? You mean you really think you can beat him?
Tortoise:	Slow and steady wins the race. That's what Grandpa always says. See you tomorrow, guys.
Action:	*All exit.*

Scene 2

Action: *Tommy Tortoise and Harry Hare are onstage.*

Tortoise: Good morning, Harry. I hope you had a good night's sleep.

Hare: I don't need that to beat **you.** *(Pauses.)* What are you doing, anyway?

Tortoise: I'm getting myself ready for the race. It's important to be all warmed up before starting a race.

Hare: *(Laughing.)* Race? Yeah, right. Get real, slowpoke, the best you can do is a trot!

Tortoise: I guess we'll just have to wait and see, Harry.

Hare: Whatever you say, slowpoke. C'mon, let's get started. On your mark, get set, GO! *(Hare dashes offstage.)*

Tortoise: Slow and steady, slow and steady. *(Slowly trots offstage.)*

Scene 3

Action: *Sammy Squirrel is operating a canteen.*

Squirrel: Oh, I think that's Harry coming. I'll just get him a nice glass of cold water. He'll probably need it with all that fast running he's doing. *(Waves to Harry Hare as he arrives onstage.)* Hey, Harry, I've got some nice cold water for you.

Hare: Water? Blaagh. Nobody drinks water these days!

Squirrel: *(Quietly.)* I drink water. So do Stephen and Tommy.

Hare: *(Laughing.)* Just what I said. Nobody drinks water these days! Give me some pop!

Squirrel: Um, Harry, I don't think it's a good idea to drink pop while you're running …

Hare: *(Loudly.)* I said I want pop!

Squirrel: Alright, Harry, here you go. *(Hands him a can of pop.)* But don't drink it too fast …

Hare: *(Drinking quickly.)* Glug, glug, glug. Ahhhh! That was … Burp! Oh, excuse me … Burp! I guess I did drink it a little too fast … **Burp!** *(Looks offstage.)* Oh, oh … Burp! Here comes that slowpoke … Burp! Tortoise. I'd better run! *(Exits stage while burping.)*

Tortoise: *(Arriving onstage.)* Slow and steady, slow and steady …

Squirrel: Hi Tommy! I've got some nice cold water for you!

Tortoise: Great, Sammy. I could really use a drink right now.

Squirrel: *(Hands him a cup.)* But don't drink it too …

Tortoise:	Fast. I know. That might give me a tummy ache.
Squirrel:	Right you are, Tommy! Good luck. Keep going!
Tortoise:	Thanks, Sammy. Slow and steady, slow and steady. *(Exits.)*

Scene 4

Action:	*Stephen Skunk is operating a canteen.*
Skunk:	Gee, I think that's Harry coming up the road. I'd better get these snacks ready. I have some carrots for Harry, and some lettuce for Tommy. I'll just get it …
Hare:	*(Races onto stage.)* Hey, stinky poo, whatcha got there?
Skunk:	I've got some snacks for you and Tommy. I have lettuce for Tommy, and I have some carrots for you.
Hare:	Carrots! I'm famished! I need more than carrots!
Skunk:	But Harry, you don't want to eat a lot during a race …
Hare:	What race? That tortoise is so far behind me I could walk the rest of the way and still win! Now, let me see. I know! I'll have a pizza!
Skunk:	Harry, I don't have pizza here.
Hare:	Well, order me one, then. Let's see, I want pepperoni, sausage and mushrooms!
Skunk:	But Harry, that'll take at least 30 minutes. You're in the middle of a race.
Hare:	There's a new place in town called "Fast or it's Free!" Call them now! *(Stephen Skunk makes telephone call, delivery raccoon arrives with pizza.)*
Skunk:	Thanks, Ricky. Wow, that was fast! Now, let me get you a piece of …
Hare:	*(Pushes past Skunk, grabs pizza and eats it noisily.)* MMMgrph. That was good!
Skunk:	Harry, you shouldn't have eaten the whole thing. You won't be able to run at all.
Hare:	*(Starts to run.)* Can too! See? I could outrun any of you! *(Runs offstage.)*
Tortoise:	*(Enters onstage.)* Hey, Stephen! How are you doing?
Skunk:	Great, Tommy! I've got some lettuce for you!
Tortoise:	That sounds good. I could use a little snack right now. But just a little … I'm running a race, you know.
Skunk:	*(Giving lettuce.)* Here you go, Tommy. Enjoy.
Tortoise:	*(Slowly chewing.)* Mmm, mmm. That was good. Guess I'd better get back in the race, though … *(Exits.)* See you, Stephen!

Skunk:	See you, Tommy! Good luck!

Scene 5

Action:	*Finish line is in sight, Harry Hare races onstage, looking sickly.*
Hare:	*(Gasping for breath.)* Oh, the finish line is just ahead … Ooooh, I feel awful. I've got a tummy ache. Maybe I can just stop and rest for a little while. I'm sure that slowpoke is **way** behind me. *(Curls up for a rest.)*
Tortoise:	*(Arrives onstage.)* Slow and steady, slow and steady. *(Walks past Hare.)* Tsk, tsk. Poor Harry. I think the pop and the pizza did him in. I'll just let him rest here. *(Moves past Hare.)* Slow and steady, slow and steady …
Hare:	*(Wakes up as Tommy Tortoise is approaching finish line.)* Oh no! That slowpoke tortoise is almost at the finish line. I'd better …
Action:	*Tommy Tortoise crosses the finish line, loud announcement is heard.*
	… AND THE WINNER … TOMMY TORTOISE!
Tortoise:	*(As Hare arrives.)* Hey, Harry, I hope you're feeling a little better.
Hare:	Er, um, well, congratulations, Tommy.
Tortoise:	Gee, thanks, Harry.
Action:	*Sammy Squirrel and Stephen Skunk arrive.*
Squirrel:	Wow, Tommy, that was great!
Skunk:	Yeah, Tommy, way to go!
Tortoise:	Thanks, guys. Hey, why don't we all go out to celebrate? You, too, Harry!
Hare:	Really? Gee, thanks. That's really nice of you, especially after all the things I said about you.
Tortoise:	That's okay. Come on, let's go.
Hare:	Where are we going?
Squirrel & Skunk:	*(Together.)* FOR PIZZA!
Action:	*Harry Hare groans, all exit.*

Concession Stand 1–Enlarge to desired size. Photocopy, color, cut out and mount on cardboard.

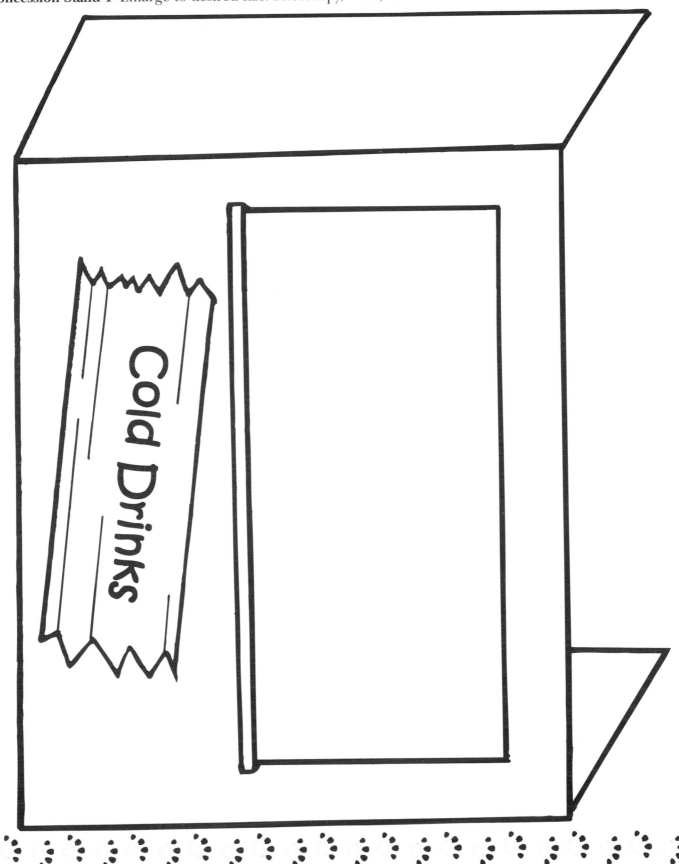

Concession Stand 2–Enlarge to desired size. Photocopy, color, cut out and mount on cardboard.

Light Snacks

Can of Soda Pop–Photocopy, color, cut out and mount on a stick.
Cup of Water–Photocopy, color, cut out and mount on a stick.
Lettuce–Photocopy, color, cut out and mount on a stick.

Pizza–Photocopy, color, cut out and mount on a stick.

The Town Mouse and the Country Mouse

Number of Puppets: 4 • Town Mouse (p. 74) • Country Mouse (p. 74) • Cat (p. 69) • Dog (p. 71) **Playing Time:** 10–15 minutes	**Props:** • small plate with crumbs (p. 50) • table set with feast (p. 51) **Music:** For scenes with Country Mouse, use country music, especially with fiddle or banjo. For scenes with Town Mouse, classical music would suit well.

Scene 1

Action:	*Music. Town Mouse enters onstage.*
Town Mouse:	*(Enters.)* Hello! Hello! Are you here, cousin? Just look at this mess. I can't believe my cousin would rather live in a barn than in a nice cozy city house like mine. Hello! Hello!
Country Mouse:	*(Enters.)* Is that you, cousin? I can't believe it! After all these years you've decided to come visit me. Come in, come in. Welcome to my humble abode.
Town Mouse:	Yes, thank you. *(Looking around.)* My, it sure is rustic, I'd say.
Country Mouse:	Rustic? Well, there's a little bit of rust on the farm equipment, but not too bad.
Town Mouse:	No, no, I said rustic. Country-like.
Country Mouse:	It sure is! I've cleaned it up and made it look just as country as possible.
Town Mouse:	*(Arrogant.)* Well it sure does look country. Hasn't changed much since I lived here years ago. Rather cold, too.
Country Mouse:	Well, there's holes in the barn walls … but they're great for coming and going.
Town Mouse:	I don't have a lot of holes in the walls where I live. There's only one door to **my** home.
Country Mouse:	Let's talk more while we're eating. I was just about to have lunch. Come and join me!
Town Mouse:	That sounds good. It's been a long journey to your place.

Country Mouse:	Here you go. Bread crumbs and wheat grains. Your favorite lunch!
Town Mouse:	No crêpes and flapjacks?
Country Mouse:	Crêpes and flapjacks? What are they? *(Hesitating.)* I do have a few cake crumbs I've been saving. Here.
Town Mouse:	Not very tasty. Honestly, I don't know how you can stay here. The barn is cold and the food is terrible. What do you do for excitement, anyway?
Country Mouse:	Oh, there's **lots** to do here. I listen to the bullfrogs singing in the pond. I watch the fireflies as they light up the farmyard at night. And in the winter the wind whistles through the trees. It's a wonderful, comforting sound.
Town Mouse:	Comforting sounds boring. And fun—you don't know what fun is. You should come to the city with me. There's always something fun to do.
Country Mouse:	Sounds pretty exciting. Maybe someday I'll go to the city to visit you, cousin.
Town Mouse:	Why someday? Why not come back to the city with me? Today!
Country Mouse:	Today? But you just got here. Aren't you going to stay with me for awhile?
Town Mouse:	Stay here? I'd freeze and starve. Come on. If we leave now we can make it home in time for supper. *(Town Mouse exits, dragging Country Mouse.)*

Scene 2

Action:	*Town Mouse and Country Mouse enter townhome.*
Town Mouse:	Here we are, cousin. Home sweet home.
Country Mouse:	It's awfully big … do you live here **alone?**
Town Mouse:	Well, **I share** the house with a people family. *(Muttering.)* And a cat and a dog.
Country Mouse:	*(Loudly.)* Did you say cat and dog?
Town Mouse:	Shhhh. They might hear you. Come on, let's have some supper. *(Climbs on table.)*
Country Mouse:	*(Hesitating.)* Are you sure it's safe?
Town Mouse:	Of course it's safe. Come on, look at the food on the table. Did you ever see such a feast?
Country Mouse:	Golly gee! Look at all the food!
Town Mouse:	… and it's only just leftovers. Come on, let's eat.
Country Mouse:	Oh, I just want to sniff that cheese for a minute …

Town Mouse:	No, cousin, you have to eat **fast.**
Country Mouse:	Fast, why? Why can't we enjoy this delicious meal?
Town Mouse:	Because we only have so much time before the … *(Cat arrives behind Country Mouse)* the … the … the … the …
Country Mouse:	What's wrong, cousin?
Town Mouse:	**Cat!** Quick, run to the mouse hole! *(Exits.)*
Country Mouse:	*(Runs around stage, Cat chases.)* Cousin! I don't know where the mouse hole is! Help! *(Cat catches mouse by the tail.)* Oh, help!
Cat:	What's this? **You're** not the mouse I saw the other day. Nevertheless, I'm sure you'll be delicious …
Dog:	*(Entering.)* Bow, wow, wow! Bow, wow, wow! What's going on? I hear voices. *(Cat is startled and Country Mouse frees himself, hides in corner of stage.)*
Cat:	Meeeow! How many times do I have to tell you … Don't sneak up on me like that!
Dog:	Bow, wow, wow. Don't tell me what to do.
Action:	*Cat and Dog begin chasing and fighting, loud barks and meows are heard, sounds of breaking dishes, dog and cat go offstage.*
Country Mouse:	Phew, that was close! My tiny little heart is beating like a drum. I've **never** been so scared!
Town Mouse:	*(Enters opposite side.)* Pssst. Cousin! Over here. My mouse hole is over here.
Country Mouse:	… and a fine time to tell me **now** where your mouse hole is. Where **were** you?
Town Mouse:	In my mouse hole, of course. Is all the fun over?
Country Mouse:	Fun? You call that fun? I nearly got eaten! You ran like a chicken and you didn't even try to help me. Is this your idea of fun?
Town Mouse:	*(Giggling.)* Yes, it is pretty exciting, isn't it? Always full of fun, the city.
Country Mouse:	Well, if this is your idea of fun, I'll leave it. I'm going back to the country. You may find it dull and boring and rusting …
Town Mouse:	… rustic.
Country Mouse:	… rustic, but it's home for me. I'm never coming back here. The country is my home, and that's exactly where I'm going. *(Exits.)*
Town Mouse:	… and I guess I'm a town mouse for sure. I'm staying here. *(Exits.)*

Small Plate with Crumbs–Photocopy, color, cut out and mount on a stick.

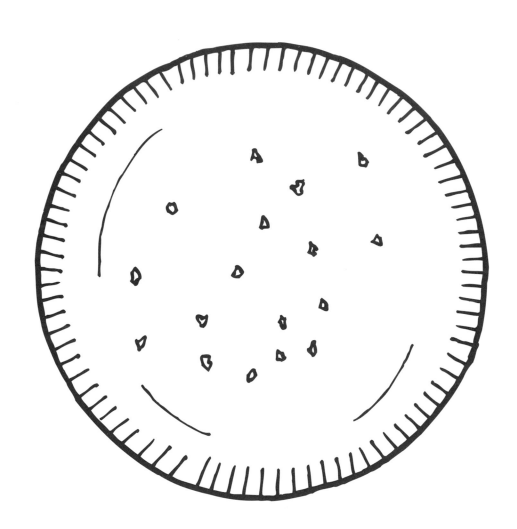

Table set with Feast–Enlarge to desired size. Photocopy, color, cut out and mount on cardboard.

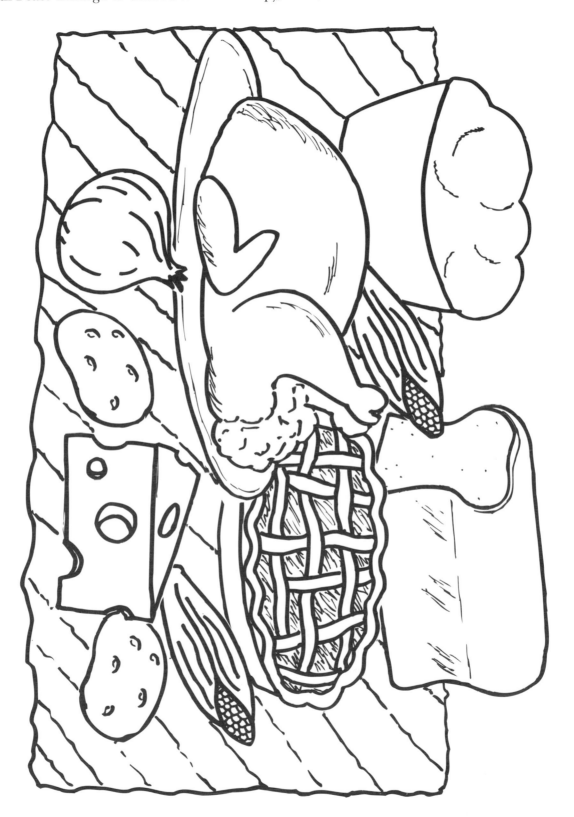

Books to Use

Bats

Batbaby Finds a Home by Robert M. Quackenbush. Random House, 2001. Batbaby and his parents search for a new home after losing the barn they had lived in. An easy-read book. See also *Batbaby* (Random House, 1997).

Bat Loves the Night by Nicola Davies, illustrations by Sarah Fox-Davies. Candlewick Press, 2001. A pipistrelle bat awakens for an evening meal.

Bats Around the Clock by Kathi Appelt, illustrations by Melissa Sweet. HarperCollins, 2000. Bats rock and roll at the American Batstand. See also *Bat Jamboree* (Scholastic, 1996).

Desert Song by Tony Johnston, illustrations by Ed Young. Candlewick Press, 2000. Various nocturnal desert animals venture out to look for food.

Hector Visits his Country Cousin by Jane Scoggins Bauld, illustrations by Gary Laronde. Eakin Press, 2002. In this third adventure in the Hector series, a city bat learns about life in the country.

Littlebat's Halloween Story by Diane Mayr, illustrations by Gideon Kendall. Albert Whitman, 2001. Littlebat listens to the stories being told below the attic where he sleeps.

A Promise to the Sun: An African Story by Tololwa M. Mollel, illustrations by Beatriz Vidal. Little, Brown and Company, 1992. A legend of why bats only come out of their caves at night.

Stellaluna by Janell Cannon. Harcourt, 1993. A baby bat is raised like a bird until she is reunited with her mother.

Bears

Baby Bear's Chairs by Jane Yolen, illustrations by Melissa Sweet. Harcourt, 2005. Baby Bear's favorite chair is in his father's lap, just before bedtime.

Ballerina Bear by Shana Corey, costume and set design by Pamela Paparone. Random House, 2002. Two bears with different talents perform together in a ballet school recital.

The Bear Came Over to My House by Rick Walton, illustrations by James Warhola. Putnam, 2001. A bear has a series of misadventures on a trip over the mountain.

Bear Wants More by Karma Wilson, illustrations by Jane Chapman. Margaret K. McElderry Books, 2003. When spring comes, Bear is very hungry and his friends treat him to great food.

The Big Little Sneeze by Katja Reider, illustrations by Wolfgang Slawski. North-South Books, 2002. A little bear thinks he's sick because the dandelions make him sneeze.

Drawing Lessons From a Bear by David M. McPhail. Little, Brown and Company, 2000. A bear explains how he became an artist.

Goldilocks Returns by Lisa Campbell Ernst. Simon & Schuster, 2000. Goldilocks returns to the bears' house 30 years later to soothe her guilty conscience.

Happy Birthday, Jesse Bear! by Nancy White Carlstrom, illustrations by Bruce Degen. Aladdin Paperbacks, 2000. Rhyming text and illustrations describe Jesse Bear's birthday party.

Hold Tight! by John Prater. Barron's, 2003. Grandfather Bear takes a break from his chores to play with Baby Bear.

Mama's Little Bears by Nancy Tafuri. Scholastic, 2002. Little bears explore their forest while staying close to Mama.

My Friend Bear by Jez Alborough. Candlewick Press, 2001. Eddie and his teddy bear meet a very big bear in the woods.

No Trouble at All by Sally Grindley. Bloomsbury Children's Books, 2002. Grandfather Bear thinks his cubs are wonderful and can't imagine them being naughty.

Oliver Finds His Way by Phyllis Root, illustrations by Christopher Denise. Candlewick Press, 2002. Oliver the bear becomes lost but comes up with a clever idea to find his way back home.

Papa's Song by Kate McMullan, illustrations by Jim McMullan. Farrar, Straus and Giroux, 2000. After Grandma, Grandpa and Mama Bear try to sing Baby Bear to sleep, Papa finds just the right song.

A Perfect Day for It by Jan Fearnley. Harcourt, 2002. Bear announces that it's "a perfect day for it" and his friends wonder what "it" is.

Polar Bolero: A Bedtime Dance by Debi Gliori. Harcourt, 2001. A polar bear is too hot to sleep and decides to go outside for a nighttime dance.

Sleep Tight, Little Bear! by Martin Waddell, illustrations by Barbara Firth. Candlewick Press, 2005. Little Bear finds a new place to sleep all by himself, but will Big Bear be alright without him?

Snow Bear by Jean Craighead George, illustrations by Wendell Minor. Hyperion, 2002. Bessie and a polar bear cub play on the ice together.

Snow Bears by Martin Waddell, illustrations by Sarah Fox-Davies. Candlewick Press, 2003. Three little bears play in the snow.

Stay Awake, Bear! by Gavin Bishop. Orchard Books, 2000. Two bears decide unsuccessfully to stay awake all winter.

A Story for Bear by Dennis Haseley, illustrations by Jim LaMarche. Silver Whistle, 2002. A young bear is fascinated by the markings on paper and he finds a friend when a kind woman reads to him.

Teddy Bear, Teddy Bear by Alice Schertle, illustrations by Linda Hill Griffith. HarperCollins, 2003. Cheerful poems about teddy bears.

We Are Bears by Molly Grooms. NorthWord Press, 2000. Mother bear leads her two cubs out of the den for the first time.

Where There's a Bear, There's Trouble! by Michael Catchpool, illustrations by Vanessa Cabban. Tiger Tales, 2002. One bear follows one bee, but instead of honey, he finds trouble.

Birds

Albert by Donna Jo Napoli, illustrations by Jim LaMarche. Silver Whistle, 2001. Two cardinals come to build a nest in Albert's hand.

Baby Bird's First Nest by Frank Asch. Harcourt, 1999. When Baby Bird falls from her mother's nest she finds a friend in Little Frog. See other Frank Asch books.

The Bird House by Cynthia Rylant, illustrations by Barry Moser. Blue Sky Press, 1998. An orphan girl discovers an unexpected home when she stops to admire birds flocking around a woman's house.

The Birdwatchers by Simon James. Candlewick Press, 2002. A young girl accompanies her grandfather on a bird-watching expedition.

Eaglet's World by Evelyn Minshull, illustrations by Andrea Gabriel. Albert Whitman, 2002. A baby bald eagle hesitates to leave his parents' nest.

Fly! by Christopher Myers. Hyperion, 2001. A homeless man teaches Jawanza how to make friends with the birds.

Jack and Jim by Kitty Crowther. Hyperion, 2000. A blackbird and a seagull become friends.

Little Bird and the Moon Sandwich by Linda Berkowitz. Crown Publishers, 1998. When they see the moon in the water, Little Bird, Alfonse and the other geese dive to the bottom of the pond to retrieve it.

Mole and the Baby Bird by Marjorie Newman, illustrations by Patrick Benson. Bloomsbury Children's Books, 2002. Mole rescues a baby bird and cares for it, but realizes that he must set it free.

Sparrow Jack by Mordicai Gerstein. Farrar, Straus and Giroux, 2003. The story of a man who brought sparrows to America in the 1860s.

The Strange Egg by Mary Newell DePalma. Houghton Mifflin, 2001. A little bird tries to hatch a strange egg before a monkey tells her it is an orange.

Two Blue Jays by Anne Rockwell, illustrations by Megan Halsey. Walker & Co., 2003. A classroom of children get a front row view as a pair of blue jays build a nest.

What's the Magic Word? by Kelly DiPucchio, illustrations by Marsha Winborn. HarperCollins, 2004. A newly-hatched bird tries to find a home by using different animal passwords.

Will You Be My Friend? A Bunny and Bird Story by Nancy Tafuri. Scholastic, 2000. A bunny helps Bird rebuild her nest and shows her what a good friend can be.

Cats

The Cat Who Liked Potato Soup by Terry Farish, illustrations by Barry Root. Candlewick Press, 2003. An old man and a cat share each other's company.

The Cat Who Loved Mozart by Patricia Austin, illustrations by Henri Sorensen. Holiday House, 2001. Jennifer's new cat Amadeus is not too friendly until he hears her playing Mozart on the piano.

Clever Cat by Peter Collington. Knopf, 2000. When Mr. and Mrs. Ford discover that their cat can get his own food, they give him a house key and a credit card.

Come Along, Kitten by Joanne Ryder, illustrations by Susan Winter. Simon & Schuster, 2003. A simple rhyming picture book of a kitten exploring its world.

Desser the Best Ever Cat by Maggie Smith. Dell Dragonfly Books, 2001. A child recounts the life and death of a favorite cat.

Excuse Me—Are You a Witch? by Emily Horn, illustrations by Pawel Pawlak. Charlesbridge Publishing, 2004. A lonely black cat named Herbert searches for some witches to keep him company.

Ginger Finds a Home by Charlotte Voake. Candlewick Press, 2003. A stray cat finds a home with a loving little girl. See also *Ginger* (Candlewick Press, 1997) and *Pizza Kittens* (Candlewick Press, 2002).

Have You Got My Purr? by Judy West, illustrations by Tim Warnes. Dutton Children's Books, 2000. When a little kitten can't purr, she asks the other animals about it.

Holly: The True Story of a Cat by Ruth Brown. Henry Holt & Company, 2000. A kitten is taken in by a loving family at Christmas.

How the Cat Swallowed Thunder by Lloyd Alexander, illustrations by Judith Byron Schachner. Dutton Children's Books, 2000. A cat tries to clean up the mess he has made while Mother Holly is away.

A Kitten Called Moonlight by Martin Waddell, illustrations by Christian Birmingham. Candlewick Press, 2001. A little girl and her mother recount the story of how a special kitten came into their lives.

A Kitten's Year by Nancy Day, illustrations by Anne Mortimer. HarperCollins, 2000. A kitten playfully grows into a cat through the year.

Little Spotted Cat by Alyssa Satin Capucilli, illustrations by Dan Andreasen. Dial, 2005. Little Spotted Cat gets into all sorts of mischief when he decides to play rather than take his nap.

Meow: Cat Stories from Around the World by Jane Yolen, illustrations by Hala Wittwer. HarperCollins, 2005. Cat tales from different countries.

Mrs. McTats and Her Houseful of Cats by Alyssa Capucilli, illustrations by Joan Rankin. Margaret K. McElderry Books, 2001. A woman with a cat makes room for 24 more cats and a puppy.

My Cat Just Sleeps by Joanne Partis. Oxford University Press, 2003. A little girl wonders why all her cat does is sleep.

Opera Cat by Tess Weaver, illustrations by Andréa Wesson. Clarion Books, 2002. When an opera singer gets laryngitis, her singing cat fills in.

Sneakers the Seaside Cat by Margaret Wise Brown, illustrations by Anne Mortimer. HarperCollins, 2003. Sneakers's first trip to the seaside proves to be an adventure.

Stella's Dancing Days by Sandy Asher, illustrations by Kathryn Brown. Harcourt, 2001. A dancing cat grows tired of dancing, but her six kittens carry on the tradition.

Tom's First Day of School by Beth Robbins, illustrations by Jon Stuart. DK Publishing, 2001. A young cat worries about the first day of school.

Why Not? by Mary Wormell. Farrar, Straus and Giroux, 2000. When his mother tells him not to bother the other animals, Barnaby asks "Why?"

Zat Cat! A Haute Couture Tail by Chesley McLaren. Scholastic, 2002. A stray cat disrupts a Paris fashion show and creates a new style.

Chickens

A Chick Called Saturday by Joyce Dunbar, illustrations by Brita Granström. Eerdmans, 2003. Saturday the chick doesn't conform to the ideals of his mother and siblings.

Chicken Chickens by Valeri Gorbachev. North-South Books, 2001. Two little chickens are afraid of trying the slide at the playground.

Cluck, Cluck Who's There? by James Mayhew. Scholastic, 2004. Harriet the hen lays egg after egg but must wait and wait.

Crabby Cratchitt by Gregory Maguire, illustrations by Andrew Glass. Clarion Books, 2000. A clucking hen nearly ends up in the frying pan.

Daisy Comes Home by Jan Brett. Putnam, 2002. An unhappy hen has a river adventure.

Dora's Eggs by Julie Sykes, illustrations by Jane Chapman. Tiger Tales, 2002. Dora thinks all of the farm animals' babies are more beautiful than her eggs ... until they hatch.

Hedgie's Surprise by Jan Brett. Putnam, 2000. A hedgehog helps a hen trick the Tomten who has been stealing her eggs.

Hungry Hen by Richard Waring, illustrations by Caroline Jayne Church. Oxford University Press, 2001. A greedy fox waits for a fattening hen to be just right.

Little Chick's Happy Easter by Wendy Cheyette Lewison, illustrations by Debra Ziss. Scholastic, 2002. A rhyming story of Little Chick's surprise for his mother.

Little Joe's Big Race by Andy Blackford, illustrations by Tim Archbold. Franklin Watts, 2000. Little Joe carries the egg and spoon from a race until the egg hatches.

Minerva Louise and the Red Truck by Janet Morgan Stoeke. Dutton Children's Books, 2002. A hen joyrides on the back of a truck.

Mrs. Chicken and the Hungry Crocodile by Won-Ldy Paye and Margaret H. Lippert, illustrations by Julie Paschkis. Henry Holt & Company, 2003. A chicken who is not satisfied with the small reflection she can see in a puddle, makes her way to the river where a hungry crocodile waits.

Queenie, One of the Family by Bob Graham. Candlewick Press, 2001. A girl and her parents rescue a hen from a lake.

The Scarecrow's Hat by Ken Brown. Peachtree Publishers, 2001. A chicken must do some bartering to get Scarecrow's nice hat for a nest.

Silly Chicken by Rukhsana Khan, illustrations by Yunmee Kyong. Viking Penguin, 2005. Rani believes that her mother loves their pet chicken more than her, until the day that a fluffy chick appears and steals Rani's own affections.

Something Wonderful by Jenny Nimmo, illustrations by Debbie Boon. Harcourt, 2001. A little hen proves herself on a farm full of skeptical chickens.

This Little Chick by John Lawrence. Candlewick Press, 2002. A little chick imitates the sounds of the animals in his neighborhood.

We're Going on a Picnic! by Pat Hutchins. Greenwillow Books, 2002. Hen, Duck and Goose have trouble deciding where to have their picnic.

What's Cooking, Jamela? by Niki Daly. Farrar, Straus and Giroux, 2001. Jamela is supposed to fatten up a chicken

for Christmas, but she gives it a name and makes it her friend.

Cows

And the Cow Said Moo! by Mildred Phillips, illustrations by Sonja Lamut. Greenwillow Books, 2000. A cow questions why other animals make their own sounds instead of saying "moo."

Click, Clack, Moo: Cows that Type by Doreen Cronin, illustrations by Betsy Lewin. Simon & Schuster, 2000. Farmer Brown's cows discover a typewriter in the barn and start making demands.

Cows Can't Fly by David Milgrim. Puffin, 2000. A child tries to convince others that cows can fly when a drawing of one is blown away by a breeze.

How to Speak Moo! by Deborah Fajerman. Random House, 2002. All cows say is "moo," but how they say it means a lot.

Kiss the Cow by Phyllis Root, illustrations by Will Hillenbrand. Candlewick Press, 2000. The family cow is upset when Annalisa refuses to kiss it before milking it.

Minnie and Moo and the Musk of Zorro by Denys Cazet. DK Publishing, 2000. Cows masquerade as Zorro to protect their barnyard.

Moo Cow Kaboom! by Thacher Hurd. HarperCollins, 2003. A romp to space and back with an abducted cow and some aliens.

Sixteen Cows by Lisa Wheeler, illustrations by Kurt Cyrus. Harcourt, 2002. The cows of neighboring ranches get mixed up in a storm.

The Tiny, Tiny Boy and the Big, Big Cow by Nancy Van Laan, illustrations by Marjorie Priceman. Dragonfly Books, 2000. A cumulative story of a little boy trying to milk a large cow.

Where's Mary's Hat? by Stephane Barroux. Viking, 2003. A cow asks all the animals if they have seen her hat. No one has seen it—until she asks bear, who has a new kite.

Crocodiles and Alligators

Alberto the Dancing Alligator by Richard Waring, illustrations by Holly Swain. Candlewick Press, 2002. After Alberto alligator accidentally goes down the toilet, Tina seeks to save him from the city's alligator hunters.

The Christmas Crocodile by Bonny Becker, illustrations by David Small. Aladdin, 2001. A very hungry crocodile is mistakenly delivered to the wrong address at Christmas.

Crocodile: Disappearing Dragon by Jonathan London, illustrations by Paul Morin. Candlewick Press, 2001. Depicts the life of a crocodile in a southern mangrove swamp.

Crocodile Listens by April Pulley Sayre, illustrations by JoEllen McAllister Stammen. Greenwillow Books, 2001. A hungry crocodile waits for a special sound from her nesting place. Includes factual information about Nile crocodiles.

Egad, Alligator! by Harriet Ziefert, illustrations by Todd McKie. Houghton Mifflin, 2002. An alligator tries to make friends, but all the animals run away.

Guji Guji by Chih-Yuan Chen. Kane/Miller, 2004. Crocodile Guji Guji thinks he is a duck until he meets three crocodiles, who tell him that he isn't a duck.

I, Crocodile by Fred Marcellino. HarperCollins, 1999. A crocodile recounts his life after being captured by Napoleon.

Keeper of the Swamp by Ann Garrett, illustrations by Karen Chandler. Turtle Books, 1999. A boy learns from his dying Grandfather the ways of the swamp.

Meet Mr. and Mrs. Green by Keith Baker. Harcourt, 2002. A loving alligator couple enjoy doing things together.

Mrs. Chicken and the Hungry Crocodile by Won-Ldy Paye and Margaret H. Lippert. Henry Holt & Company, 2003. A chicken who is not satisfied with the small reflection she can see in a puddle, makes her way to the river where a hungry crocodile waits.

Snow Day! by Pat Lakin, illustrations by Scott Nash. Dial, 2002. Four crocodile friends play in the snow.

Very Boring Alligator by Jean Gralley. Henry Holt & Company, 2001. Simple rhymes describe an alligator who comes to play but won't leave.

Where's Your Smile, Crocodile? by Claire Freedman, illustrations by Sean Julian. Peachtree Publishers, 2001. Kyle the crocodile loses his smile, but when he helps Little Lion Cub find his way home he finds his smile.

Dogs

Benny by Sieb Posthuma. Kane/Miller, 2003. Benny the dog has lost his sense of smell.

Buster by Denise Fleming. Henry Holt & Company, 2003. Buster is a happy dog ... until a cat is brought home.

Can't You Sleep, Dotty? by Tim Warnes. Tiger Tales, 2003. Dotty the dog can't sleep in her new home until her friends come up with an idea.

A Day in the Life of Murphy by Alice Provensen. Simon & Schuster, 2003. The adventures of a little terrier who thinks his name is "Murphy-stop-that."

Dog Eared by Amanda Harvey. Doubleday, 2002. A dog tries a number of things to make his ears look better.

The Great Gracie Chase: Stop that Dog! by Cynthia Rylant, illustrations by Mark Teague. Blue Sky Press, 2001. A cumulative tale about a dog whose quiet life is disrupted by noisy painters.

Happy Dog! by Lisa Grubb. Philomel, 2003. Jack creates an imaginary play friend pup.

McDuff Saves the Day by Rosemary Wells, illustrations by Susan Jeffers. Hyperion, 2002. When ants consume the family's food, McDuff the dog tries to find something else to eat.

McDuff's Wild Romp by Rosemary Wells, illustrations by Susan Jeffers. Hyperion, 2005. MuDuff and the old cat Purlina have a tussle over a turkey tidbit.

Muldoon by Pamela Duncan Edwards, illustrations by Henry Cole. Hyperion, 2002. Muldoon the dog works hard for the West family ... or so he thinks.

Murphy Meets the Treadmill by Harriet Ziefert, illustrations by Emily Bolam. Houghton Mifflin, 2001. Cheryl decides that her yellow Labrador is overweight and puts him on an exercise program.

No, No Jack by Ron Hirsch, illustrations by Pierre Pratt. Dial, 2002. A playful dog hides things in the closet, and the family makes him return them every time ... except for one.

The Perfect Puppy for Me! by Jane O'Connor, illustrations by Jessie Hartland. Viking, 2003. A little boy investigates a variety of dogs before selecting a puppy for his birthday gift.

Riley and Rose in the Picture by Susanna Gretz. Candlewick Press, 2005. On a rainy day Riley the dog and Rosa the cat decide to stay indoors and draw a picture together, but they have trouble agreeing on how to do it.

Ruby and Fred by Blair Lent. Henry Holt & Company, 2000. Ruby the parrot and Fred the poodle join forces to keep Chita the cat at bay.

Ruby and the Muddy Dog by Helen Stephens. Kingfisher, 2000. Dog makes a lot of messes and tries to blame them on others, but Ruby convinces him that telling the truth is best.

Rufferella by Vanessa Gill-Brown. Bloomsbury Children's Books, 2000. A girl tries to turn her dog into Cinderella with mixed results.

That New Animal by Emily Jenkins, illustrations by Perre Pratt. Farrar, Straus and Giroux, 2005. The lives of two dogs change after a new animal, a baby, comes to their house.

That's My Dog! by Rick Walton, illustrations by Julia Gorton. Putnam, 2001. A red, muddy, bouncy, slobbery, stinky dog is praised by his proud owner.

This Is the Dog by Sheryl McFarlane, illustrations by Chrissie Wysotski. Fitzhenry & Whiteside, 2003. An escaped pup causes mayhem in this "House that Jack Built" type of rhyme.

Unlovable by Dan Yaccarino. Henry Holt & Company, 2001. A pug dog is made to feel inferior by a cat, a parrot and other dogs, until a new dog helps him realize he is fine the way he is.

Yip! Snap! Yap! by Charles Fuge. Tricycle Press, 2001. Different dogs make different sounds, encouraging the reader to join in.

Ducks

Baby Duck's New Friend by Frank Asch. Harcourt, 2001. Baby Duck wanders away from home, not realizing that he must find his way back.

A Cake for Herbie by Petra Mathers. Atheneum, 2000. Herbie writes poems about food for a contest and although he doesn't win, he does find an appreciative audience.

Cold Little Duck, Duck, Duck by Lisa Westberg Peters, illustrations by Sam Williams. Greenwillow Books, 2000. A little duck arrives at her pond and finds it frozen.

Do Like a Duck Does by Judy Hindley, illustrations by Ivan Bates. Candlewick Press, 2002. A mother duck challenges a stranger to imitate a duck's behavior and proves that he is a fox.

Duck on a Bike by David Shannon. Blue Sky Press, 2002. A duck learns to ride a bike and soon all the animals on the farm are doing the same.

Earthquack! by Margie Palatini, illustrations by Barry Moser. Simon & Schuster, 2002. In an inspired take on Henny Penny, Chucky Ducky thinks the earth is quaking.

Fix-It Duck by Jez Alborough. HarperCollins, 2002. Duck tries to make minor repairs and causes mayhem.

Giggle, Giggle, Quack by Doreen Cronin, illustrations by Betsy Lewin. Simon & Schuster, 2002. Duck makes trouble for Farmer Brown's brother when he is left in charge of the farm. A sequel to *Click, Clack, Moo*.

Goodnight, My Duckling by Nancy Tafuri. Scholastic, 2005. A mother duck leads her ducklings home, but one dawdles behind.

Little Quack by Lauren Thompson, illustrations by Derek Anderson. Simon & Schuster, 2003. Mama Duck is surprised to learn her little ducklings don't want to leave their nest.

Little Quack's Bedtime by Lauren Thompson. Simon & Schuster, 2005. A mother duck tries to persuade her five ducklings to go to sleep on a dark night.

Make the Team, Baby Duck! by Amy Hest, illustrations by Jill Barton. Candlewick Press, 2002. An encouraging grandfather helps Baby Duck get into the pool with the swim team.

Mucky Duck by Sally Grindley, illustrations by Neal Layton. Bloomsbury, 2003. A duck loves to get dirty.

The Nutquacker by Mary Jane Auch. Holiday House, 1999. Clara the duck puts herself in danger when she tries to discover the farm animals' secret of Christmas.

One Duck Stuck by Phyllis Root, illustrations by Jane Chapman. Candlewick Press, 1998. A counting book about a duck stuck in a marsh and the animals that try to help.

Quack and Count by Keith Baker. Harcourt, 1999. Seven ducklings look at addition in this rhyming text.

The Sissy Duckling by Harvey Fierstein, illustrations by Henry Cole. Simon & Schuster, 2002. Elmer the duck is teased for being different, but he learns to prove himself.

Webster J. Duck by Martin Waddell, illustrations by David Parkins. Candlewick Press, 2001. Webster J. Duck enlists the help of several animals in finding his mother.

Elephants

Elefantina's Dream by X. J. Kennedy, illustrations by Graham Percy. Philomel Books, 2002. Elefantina the elephant trains hard for the Elympic ice skating team, with help from a mouse.

Elephants on Board by Suse MacDonald. Harcourt, 1999. Elephants on their way to a show have a flat tire.

Ella Takes the Cake by Carmela D'Amico. Scholastic, 2005. Ella the elephant wants to help in her mother's bakery, but will the job she takes on prove to be more than she can handle?

The Goose Who Went Off in a Huff by Paul Brett Johnson. Orchard Books, 2001. A goose who wishes to be a mother gets her wish when a baby elephant is left behind by a circus.

How the Elephant Got His Trunk: A Retelling of the Rudyard Kipling Tale retold by Jean Richards, illustrations by Norman Gorbaty. Henry Holt & Company, 2003. A simplified version of Kipling's classic.

Little Elephant's Song by Wolfram Hänel, illustrations by Kristinah Kadmon. North-South Books, 2000. Baby elephant tries to master the trumpeting sound with his trunk. See also *Little Elephant Runs Away* (North-South Books, 2001).

The Mightiest by Keiko Kasza. Putnam, 2001. Lion, Bear and Elephant compete to see who can scare an old woman, but she has a surprise for them.

My Friend Harry by Kim Lewis. Candlewick Press, 1997. A young boy takes his stuffed elephant everywhere with him.

Otto's Trunk by Sandy Turner. HarperCollins, 2003. Otto is teased for his small trunk, and tries many ways to help it grow.

Splash! by Flora McDonnell. Candlewick Press, 1999. Little elephant has a good solution to a hot day for the jungle animals.

Squeak's Good Idea by Max Eilenberg, illustrations by Patrick Benson. Candlewick Press, 2001. Squeak the elephant is prepared for any eventuality when he goes outside for a picnic.

What the Elephant Told by Barbara Brenner, illustrations by Akemi Gutierrez. Henry Holt & Company, 2003. A boy and an elephant meet and spend time together.

Fish

Carl Caught a Flying Fish by Kevin O'Malley. Simon & Schuster, 1996. Carl throws back a flying fish he caught because it gives him nothing but trouble.

Cats Are Like That by Martha Weston. Holiday House, 1999. Dot tries to get her new pet fish to do something interesting while she defends them from her cat.

Clara and Asha by Eric Rohmann. Roaring Brook Press, 2005. Young Clara would rather play with her imaginary giant fish, Asha, than settle down to sleep.

Fish and Flamingo by Nancy White Carlstrom, illustrations by Lisa Desimini. Little, Brown and Company, 1993. A fish and a flamingo become good friends.

A Fish Named Spot by Jennifer P. Goldfinger. Little, Brown and Company, 2001. When he feeds his pet fish dog biscuits, Simon's wish for a dog comes true in a most unusual way.

Just Keep Swimming by Melissa Lagonegro. Random House, 2005. When Nemo worries that his too-small fin will keep him off the school swim team, his friend Dory encourages him.

Little Fish Lost by Nancy Van Laan, illustrations by Jane Conteh-Morgan. Atheneum, 1998. A little fish searches for his mother in an African pond.

Minas and the Fish by Olga Pastuchiv. Houghton Mifflin, 1997. A young boy wants to learn to swim, but when a magic fish teaches him, his brothers no longer recognize him.

One Nighttime Sea: An Ocean Counting Rhyme by Deborah Lee Rose, illustrations by Steve Jenkins. Scholastic, 2003. A rhyming counting book featuring many ocean creatures. A companion to *Into the A, B, Sea* (Scholastic, 2000).

Rainbow Fish and the Sea Monster's Cave by Marcus Pfister. North-South Books, 2001. Rainbow Fish volunteers to find healing algae in a dangerous place for a sick fish. See also *Rainbow Fish to the Rescue!* (North-South Books, 1995) and *The Rainbow Fish* (Scholastic, 1993).

Salmon Forest by David Suzuki and Sarah Ellis, illustrations by Sheena Lott. Graystone Books, 2003. A young girl learns about the life cycle of the sockeye salmon while walking with her father.

Splashy Fins, Flashy Skins: Deep Sea Rhymes to Make You Grin by Cynthia L. Copeland and Alexandra P. Lewis. Millbrook Press, 2003. Various sea creatures are represented in photo and rhyme.

A Star at the Bottom of the Sea by Gayle Ridinger, illustrations by Andreina Parpajola. Gareth Stevens, 2002. With help from her undersea friends, a starfish travels to the sky where she wants to shine and dance like the other stars, but she quickly discovers that things are not always as they appear.

Surprise Party: The Copycat Fish by Gail Donovan, illustrations by David Austin Clar. Night Sky Books, 2003. Miss Cuttie's class organizes a surprise party for her. See also *SOS, Save our Shortcut!* (Night Sky Books, 2002), *Ready,*

Set, Swim! (Night Sky Books, 2002) and *The Copycat Fish* (Night Sky Books, 2001).

Trolly Finds a Gun by Derek Savage, illustrations by Denny Bustamante. Savage Books, 2001. Trolly and his friends find a gun and they decide not to touch it. Part of the Trolly the Trout series.

Frogs

Baby Bird's First Nest by Frank Asch. Scholastic, 1999. When Baby Bird falls from her mother's nest she finds a friend in Little Frog. See other Frank Asch books.

The Big Wide-Mouthed Frog by Ana Martín Larrañaga. Candlewick Press, 1999. A frog asks every animal he meets what he or she likes to eat, but he doesn't like crocodile's answer.

Down by the Cool of the Pool by Tony Mitton, illustrations by Guy Parker-Rees. Orchard Books, 2002. Frog and friends have a dancing good time by the pool.

Five Green and Speckled Frogs by Priscilla Burris. Scholastic, 2003. A lively illustrated version of the traditional rhyme.

Fribbity Ribbit! by Suzanne C. Johnson, illustrations by Debbie Tilley. Knopf, 2001. A frog creates havoc inside a house.

Friend Frog by Alma Flor Ada, illustrations by Lori Lohstoeter. Scholastic, 2000. Field mouse wonders if he can be friends with a frog who is so different from him.

The Frog Principal by Stephanie Calmenson, illustrations by Denise Brunkus. Scholastic, 2001. A school principal is accidentally turned into a frog by a bumbling magician.

Frog by Susan Cooper, illustrations by Jane Browne. Margaret McElderry Books, 2002. A young boy learns to swim by watching a frog.

Froggy Plays in a Band by Jonathan London, illustrations by Frank Remkiewicz. Viking, 2002. Froggy's marching band practices to be in a parade. See also *Froggy's Best Christmas* (Viking, 2000), *Froggy's First Kiss* (Viking, 1998) and others.

Frog Legs: A Picture Book of Action Verse by George Shannon, illustrations by Amit Trynan. Greenwillow Books, 2000. Frog enjoys stomping, flopping, tipping and doing the boogie buggaloo.

Jubal's Wish by Audrey Wood, illustrations by Don Wood. Blue Sky Press, 2000. Jubal Bullfrog wants his friends to be happy, and happiness comes in an unexpected way.

Marsh Music by Marianne Collins Berkes, illustrations by Robert Noreika. Millbrook Press, 2000. The marsh comes alive at night with the singing of various types of frogs.

Too Many Frogs! by Sandy Asher. Penguin Putnam, 2005. Rabbit's nightly routine is disturbed by Froggie, who invites himself in for a snack and a story.

What Did I Look Like When I Was a Baby? by Jeanne Willis, illustrations by Tony Ross. Putnam, 2000. A young bullfrog is very surprised to see what he looked like as a baby.

Hippopotamuses

Dorothy and Mikey by Keiko Kasza. Putnam, 2000. Three stories feature two hippopotamus friends.

Hurty Feelings by Helen Lester. Houghton Mifflin, 2004. Fragility, a hippopotamus whose feelings are easily hurt, meets Rudy, a rude elephant.

Kiss, Kiss by Margaret Wild. Simon & Schuster, 2004. Baby Hippo is in such a rush to play one morning he forgets to kiss his mama, but strangely all the jungle noises seem to remind him.

The Little Hippos' Adventure by Lena Landström. Farrar, Straus and Giroux, 2002. Little hippos think it would be more fun if their diving board could be higher.

Naughty! by Caroline Castle, illustrations by Sam Childs. Knopf, 2001. Two naughty babies, a zebra and a hippo, get in trouble.

The Real Winner by Charise Neugebauer, illustrations by Barbara Nascimbeni. North-South Books, 2000. A competitive raccoon learns a lesson from a hippopotamus.

Ruby and the Noisy Hippo by Helen Stephens. Kingfisher, 2000. Ruby doesn't want to be with her noisy hippo friend, but when his loudness saves her from a monster she decides it's okay to be noisy sometimes.

Snarlyhissopus by Alan MacDonald, illustrations by Louise Voce. Tiger Tales, 2002. A silly wordplay game as confused animals in the jungle wait to meet a hippopotamus.

This Whole Tooth Fairy Thing's Nothing But a Big Rip-off! by Lois G. Grambling, illustrations by Thomas Payne. Marshall Cavendish, 2002. Little Hippo waits for the Tooth Fairy and ends up making a tooth-to-coin exchange for her.

Time to Go, Hippo by Bob Hartman, illustrations by Kate Simpson. Augsburg Fortress, 2002. Farmers in a rice field are baffled at how to move a hippo.

The Turtle and the Hippopotamus by Kate Banks, illustrations by Tomasz Bogacki. Farrar, Straus and Giroux, 2002. A rebus book about a turtle who won't swim across the river because she is afraid of the hippopotamus.

Mice

The Barking Mouse by Antonio Sacre, illustrations by Alfredo Aguirre. Albert Whitman, 2003. A brave mother mouse saves her family when she frightens a cat away.

Busy Busy Mouse by Virginia Kroll, illustrations by Fumi Kosaka. Viking, 2003. A mouse rests during the day while the family in the house is active, but when they go to sleep he has many things to do.

Friend Frog by Alma Flor Ada, illustrations by Lori Lohstoeter. Scholastic, 2000. Field mouse wonders if he can be friends with a frog who is so different from him.

Hide and Seek by Brenda Shannon Yee, illustrations by Debbie Tilley. Orchard Books, 2001. A mouse plays hide-and-seek with the owner of a house.

How Many Sleeps? by Amber Stewart and Layn Marlow. Oxford University Press, 2005. Toast the mouse is very excited about his upcoming birthday. Why is his father worried?

If You Take a Mouse to School by Laura Joffe Numeroff, illustrations by Felicia Bond. Laura Geringer Books, 2002. Taking a mouse to school can lead to a series of consequences. One of several Numeroff books, including *If You Take a Mouse to the Movies* (Laura Geringer Books, 2000).

I. Q. Goes to the Library by Mary Ann Fraser. Walker & Co., 2003. A mouse and his human classmates learn about their school library.

Jack and the Leprechaun by Ivan Robertson, illustrations by Katy Bratun. Random House, 2000. A little mouse visits his cousin in Ireland on St. Patrick's Day.

Little Mouse and the Big Red Apple by A. H. Benjamin, illustrations by Gwyneth Williamson. Scholastic, 2000. A mouse, struggling to carry a big apple, does not want to share with the animals who help along the way. See also *Mouse, Mole and the Falling Star* (Dutton, 2002).

The Little Mouse, the Red Ripe Strawberry and the Big Hungry Bear by Don and Audrey Wood. Child's Play, 1999. A little mouse fears that the strawberry he has picked will be taken by the bear.

Maisy Drives the Bus by Lucy Cousins. Candlewick Press, 2000. Maisy the mouse drives an assortment of passengers on her bus. One of several Maisy books.

Miss Mouse's Day by Jan Ormerod. HarperCollins, 2001. A mouse's day includes all sorts of activities, and finishes with a goodnight kiss.

Mouse by Mouse: A Counting Adventure by Julia Noonan. Dutton, 2003. Humorous illustrations depict a lonely mouse and his growing company.

Mouse Cleaning by Rose-Marie Provencher, illustrations by Bernadette Pons. Henry Holt & Company, 2001. A woman is inspired to houseclean when she discovers a mouse in her house.

Mouse Practice by Emily Arnold McCully. Scholastic, 1999. A little mouse learns from his parents that practice is the best way to succeed.

Mouse's First Spring by Lauren Thompson. Simon & Schuster, 2005. A mouse and its mother experience the delights of nature on a windy spring day.

The Mouse that Snored by Bernard Waber. Houghton Mifflin, 2000. A snoring mouse wakens the residents of a quiet house.

Thank You, Little Mouse by Dugald Steer. Backpack Books, 2005. Little Mouse always remembers to say thank you, but Gran and Grandpa are so kind that sometimes thank you doesn't seem enough. See also *Good Night Little Mouse* (Backpack Books, 2005).

Three Pebbles and a Song by Eileen Spinelli, illustrations by S. D. Schindler. Dial, 2003. Moses the mouse can't concentrate on gathering supplies for winter, but prefers to dance.

Truffle's Christmas by Anna Currey. Orchard Books, 2000. An unselfish little mouse has his Christmas wishes fulfilled by Santa.

Wemberly Worried by Kevin Henkes. Greenwillow Books, 2000. Wemberly the mouse worries about everything, including the first day of nursery school.

Monkeys

The Bird, the Monkey and the Snake in the Jungle by Kate Banks, illustrations by Tomasz Bogacki. Farrar, Straus and Giroux, 1999. A rebus story featuring three creatures searching for a new home.

Caps for Sale by Esphyr Slobodkina. HarperCollins, 2002. A cap peddler wakes from a nap to find all his caps have been taken by monkeys. No matter what he does, the monkeys only imitate him.

Five Little Monkeys with Nothing to Do by Eileen Christelow. Clarion Books, 2002. One of a series of books by Christelow about five mischievous monkeys.

See also *Five Little Monkeys Wash the Car* (Clarion, 2000), *Five Little Monkeys Jumping On the Bed* (Turtleback, 2000) and others.

Friends Again? by H. J. Arrington, illustrations by JoAnn Kitchel. Pelican, 2001. An East African folktale about a monkey who teaches a crocodile the importance of treating friends with honesty and loyalty.

Little Monkey Says Good Night by Ann Whitford Paul, illustrations by David Walker. Farrar, Straus and Giroux, 2003. Little monkey scampers to the Big Top tent, saying good night to all his friends.

Manny Monkey by Dave and Pat Sargent. Ozark Publishing, 2001. Manny Monkey finds himself safe with a friend after the circus train derails.

The Monkey Who Wanted the Moon by Anne Mangan, illustrations by Catherine Walters. Interlink Pub., 2000. A curious monkey wants to reach for all the beautiful things she sees, including the moon.

Naughty Little Monkeys by Jim Aylesworth, illustrations by Henry Cole. Dutton, 2003. An energetic alphabet book featuring mischievous monkeys.

Nestor by Quentin Gréban. Mondo Publishing, 2001. When Nestor the monkey falls into the river, he is rescued by an elephant, one of the animals his father had told him to avoid.

One Monkey Too Many by Jackie French Koller, illustrations by Lynn Munsinger. Harcourt, 1999. Adventurous monkeys enjoy a series of escapades on their vacation.

10 Little Sock Monkeys by Harriet Ziefert, illustrations by William B. Winburn. Sterling Publishing, 2005. Rhyming monkey verse with sock monkey illustrations.

Ten Monkey Jamboree by Dianne Ochiltree, illustrations by Anne-Sophie Lanquetin. Margaret K. McElderry Books, 2001. Rhyming text and illustrations demonstrate how many monkeys it takes to make a Jungle Jamboree.

Water Hole Waiting by Jane Kurtz, illustrations by Lee Christiansen. Greenwillow Books, 2001. A thirsty monkey waits his turn at the water hole on the African savanna.

When the Monkeys Came Back by Kristine Franklin, illustrations by Robert Roth. Macmillan, 1994. Remembering how the monkeys in her Costa Rican valley disappeared when the trees were cut down, Marta grows up, plants more trees and sees the return of the monkeys.

Owls

Bilby Moon by Margaret Spurling, illustrations by Danny Snell. Kane/Miller, 2001. Bilby greets the moon every night, but one night a piece of the moon is missing and he sets out to find the piece.

Goodnight Owl! by Pat Hutchins. Aladdin Books, 1990. Because all the other animals' noises keep him from sleeping, Owl watches for a chance to take his revenge.

Hoot and Holler by Alan Brown, illustrations by Rimantas Rolia. Knopf, 2001. Two owls separated by a storm discover their true feelings for each other.

The Little Brown Owl and Me by Joyce Gibbons, illustrations by Jane Lenoir. Coastal Publishing, 2001. A little boy who is lost in the woods finds his way home thanks to an owl.

The Moonlit Owl by Richard Brown, illustrations by Stephen Lambert. Cambridge University Press, 2003. One of a series of British books, this one being a trip out in the moonlight.

Owl Babies by Martin Waddell, illustrations by Patrick Benson. Candlewick Press, 2002. Three owl babies wait for their mother's return.

The Owl Who Was Afraid of the Dark by Jill Tomlinson, illustrations by Paul Howard. Candlewick Press, 2001. A Mommy owl teaches her frightened little one the pleasures of the evening.

Owly by Mike Thaler, illustrations by David Wiesner. Walker, 1998. When Owly asks his mother question after question about the world, she finds ways to answer his requests.

Pigs

Can You Make a Piggy Giggle? by Linda Ashman, illustrations by Henry Cole. Dutton, 2002. Rhymed suggestions for making a pig giggle.

Dumpy La Rue by Elizabeth Winthrop, illustrations by Betsy Lewin. Henry Holt & Company, 2001. A rhyming story about a pig who loves to dance.

The Good Little Bad Little Pig by Margaret Wise Brown, illustrations by Dan Yaccarino. Hyperion, 2002. Peter's wish comes true when he gets a little pet pig who is sometimes good and sometimes bad.

The Great Pig Search by Eileen Christelow. Clarion Books, 2001. Bert and Ethel go to Florida to look for their runaway pigs and find them in surprising places.

If You Give a Pig a Pancake by Laura Joffe Numeroff, illustrations by Felicia Bond. Scholastic, 1998. One thing leads to another when you give a pig a pancake.

Little Flower by Gloria Rand, illustrations by R. W. Alley. Henry Holt & Company, 2002. When Miss Pearl falls and breaks her hip, her potbellied pig goes for help.

Little Pig Figwort Can't Get to Sleep by Henrietta Branford, illustrations by Claudio Muñoz. Clarion Books, 2000. Little Pig Figwort can't sleep so he goes off to the North Pole, the moon and the bottom of the sea.

Little Pig is Capable by Denis Roche. Houghton Mifflin, 2002. Little Pig's parents worry about him to an unusual degree.

Mortimer Mooner Stopped Taking a Bath by Frank B. Edwards and John Bianchi. Pokeweed Press, 2000. A young pig becomes dirtier and dirtier.

Mrs. Pig's Night Out by Ros Asquith, illustrations by Selina Young. Trafalgar, 2003. Mr. Pig watches over his three children as Mrs. Pig gets a night out.

Pablo the Pig by Bruno Hächler, illustrations by Nina Spranger. North-South Books, 2002. Pablo the pig's life is endangered, but his friend Vera helps save him.

Patsy Says by Leslie Tryon. Atheneum, 2000. Patsy Pig is determined to teach Ms. Klingensmith's class some manners.

Piggy and Dad Go Fishing by David Martin, illustrations by Frank Remkiewicz. Candlewick Press, 2005. Piggy goes fishing with his dad, but he feels sorry for the fish and the worms.

Piggy's Belly Button by Keith Faulkner, illustrations by Jonathan Lambert. Random House, 2003. Piggy's mother warns him not to push his belly button, but he doesn't listen.

Piggy's Pancake Parlor by David M. McPhail. Dutton, 2002. Piggy and Fox open a restaurant where they serve special pancakes. See also *Pigs Aplenty, Pigs Galore!* (Dutton, 1993) and *Pigs Ahoy!* (Dutton, 1995).

Piglet and Mama by Margaret Wild. H. N. Abrams, 2004. When Piglet cannot find her mother, all of the barnyard animals try to make her feel better.

Pigs Rock! by Melanie Davis Jones, illustrations by Bob Staake. Viking, 2003. A musical band of pigs play various kinds of music for their fans.

Pirate Piggy Wiggy by Christyan and Diane Fox. Handprint, 2003. PiggyWiggy embarks on an imagi-

nary sailing adventure. See also *Fire Fighter PiggyWiggy* (Handprint, 2001) and *Astronaut PiggyWiggy* (Handprint, 2002).

Six Hogs on a Scooter by Eileen Spinelli, illustrations by Scott Nash. Orchard Books, 2000. The Hog family try to make it to the opera using various modes of transportation.

Toot and Puddle: Top of the World by Holly Hobbie. Little, Brown and Company, 2002. When Toot takes a long walk his friend Puddle sets out to find him.

The True Story of the 3 Little Pigs by Jon Scieszka, illustrations by Lane Smith. Puffin, 1997. The wolf gives his own version of what happened to the three little pigs.

Wait! No Paint! by Bruce Whatley. HarperCollins, 2001. The three little pigs get a little mixed up with the help of a mysterious voice.

When You Take a Pig to a Party by Kristina Thermaenius McLarey, illustrations by Marjory Wunsch. Orchard Books, 2000. Havoc ensues when a pig is taken to a friend's birthday party.

Rabbits

A Boy and his Bunny by Sean Bryan, illustrations by Tom Murphy. Arcade Pub., 2005. A boy wakes up with a rabbit on his head and discovers he can still do just about anything.

Bunny Isabel's Easter Egg Hunt by Max Haynes. Dutton, 1998. A lift-the-flap book in which Bunny helps Mother Hen search for her egg.

Bunny, My Honey by Anita Jeram. Candlewick Press, 2001. A little lost bunny wonders whether his Mother can find him. A board book.

Bunny's Noisy Book by Margaret Wise Brown, illustrations by Lisa McCue. Hyperion, 2000. A bunny listens to noises all around him and then makes some of his own.

Floppy Ears by Ruth Louise Symes, illustrations by Tony Kenyon. Orion Publishing Group, 2005. Although Floppy Ears is little, he's clever enough to outsmart the fox.

Flora's Blanket by Debi Gliori. Orchard Books, 2001. A little rabbit searches for her missing blanket with help from her family.

Grumblebunny by Bob Hartman, illustrations by David Clark. Putnam, 2003. Although his siblings are tired of his gloomy outlook, they are very glad to have him around when Wolf Peter arrives.

Happy Birthday, Davy! by Brigitte Weninger, illustrations by Eve Tharlet. North-South Books, 2000. Davy Rabbit's special wishes are fulfilled by his grandparents' visit.

Hop, Hop, Hop! by Ann Whitford Paul, illustrations by Jan Gerardi. Random House, 2005. Little Rabbit follows Big Rabbit, until he discovers that things work better if he does it his own way.

The Little Blue Rabbit by Angela McAllister, illustrations by Jason Cockcroft. Bloomsbury, 2003. Blue Rabbit, a plush toy, looks for the little boy who sleeps with him each night.

My World by Margaret Wise Brown, illustrations by Clement Hurd. HarperCollins, 2001. A little bunny delights in all the familiar things in his daily life.

Nibbles O'Hare by Betty Paraskevas, illustrations by Michael Paraskevas. Simon & Schuster, 2001. Nibbles convinces his new neighbors that he is the Easter Bunny.

Nicky and the Fantastic Birthday Gift by Valeri Gorbachev. North-South Books, 2000. A young rabbit creates an imaginative picture for his mother's birthday.

Rabbit's Wooly Sweater by Mark Birchall. Carolrhoda Books, 2001. Rabbit does not want to wear her new sweater until she has one for her toy rabbit.

Read to Your Bunny by Rosemary Wells. Scholastic, 1998. Brief rhyming text and colorful illustrations depict the importance of reading.

Ruthie's Big Old Coat by Julie Lacome. Candlewick Press, 2000. Ruthie's hand-me-down coat is just the right size for her and her friend Flora.

The Tale of Peter Rabbit by Beatrix Potter, illustrations by Michael Hague. SeaStar Books, 2001. The traditional tale of Peter Rabbit who disobeys his mother and goes into Mr. McGregor's garden.

Tiny Rabbit Goes to a Birthday Party by John Wallace. Holiday House, 2000. Tiny Rabbit worries about going to his first birthday party.

Too Big, Too Small, Just Right by Frances Minters, illustrations by Janie Bynum. Harcourt, 2001. Two rabbits looking for a new home discover a number of opposites such as big and small, short and tall and heavy and light.

Why So Sad, Brown Rabbit? by Sheridan Cain, illustrations by Jo Kelly. Puffin Books, 2001. Brown Rabbit wants a family, but three newborn ducklings are not quite what he has in mind.

Will You Be My Friend? A Bunny and Bird Story by Nancy Tafuri. Scholastic, 2000. Bunny and Bird become good friends while rebuilding Bird's ruined nest.

Raccoons

Hunter's Best Friend at School by Laura Elliott, illustrations by Lynn Munsinger. HarperCollins, 2002. Hunter the raccoon doesn't know what to do when his friend starts acting up at preschool.

The Little Raccoon by Elizabeth Ring, illustrations by Dwight Kuhn. Turtleback, 2001. A curious little raccoon spends the day exploring and eating.

Little Raccoon Always Knows Best by Käthe Recheis, illustrations by Pieter Kunstreich. Munchweiler Pr., 2002. Little Raccoon knows the best places to hunt for food, and the best hollows to sleep in.

Little Raccoon's Big Question by Miriam Schlein, illustrations by Ian Schoenherr. Greenwillow Books, 2004. When Little Raccoon asks his mother when she loves him the most, she finally answers "always right now."

Now What Can I Do? by Margaret Park Bridges, illustrations by Melissa Sweet. SeaStar Books, 2001. Little raccoon is stuck inside on a rainy day and looks for things to do.

A Pocket Full of Kisses by Audrey Penn, illustrations by Barbara Leonard Gibson. Child Welfare League of America, 2004. Chester Raccoon is worried that his mother does not have enough love for both him and his new baby brother.

Raccoon On His Own by Jim Arnosky. Putnam, 2001. A curious raccoon takes an unexpected trip in a boat.

Raccoon Tune by Nancy Shaw, illustrations by Howard Fine. Henry Holt & Company, 2003. A family of mischievous raccoons search for treats during the night.

The Real Winner by Charise Neugebauer, illustrations by Barbara Nascimbeni. North-South Books, 2000. A competitive raccoon learns a lesson from a hippopotamus.

Timothy Goes to School by Rosemary Wells. Puffin Books, 2000. Timothy learns about making friends during his first week at school.

Sheep

The Day the Sheep Showed Up by David McPhail. Scholastic, 1998. An easy reader about a sheep's arrival to the barnyard.

Delilah by John Bemelmans Marciano. Viking, 2002. Delilah the lamb's friendship with Farmer Red is threatened by the arrival of more sheep.

Farmer Brown Shears His Sheep by Teri Sloat, illustrations by Nadine Bernard Westcott. DK Publishing, 2000. Farmer Brown's recently sheared sheep beg for their wool back, so he knits the yarn into sweaters for them.

Harley by Star Livingstone, illustrations by Molly Bang. SeaStar Books, 2001. Harley the llama who becomes a guard llama protects the sheep from coyotes and befriends a cantankerous ram.

The Many Adventures of Johnny Mutton by James Proimos. Harcourt, 2001. Although he is a sheep, Johnny does many things, but remains true to himself.

Marvin Wanted More by Joseph Theobald. Trafalgar, 2003. A small sheep tries to compensate for his size by overeating.

Mouton's Impossible Dream by Anik McGrory. Harcourt, 2000. Mouton the sheep's dream of flying comes true when she is sent up in the Montgolfier brothers' hot air balloon in 1783.

Russell the Sheep by Rob Scotton. HarperCollins, 2005. Russell the sheep tries all different ways to get to sleep.

Sheep Asleep by Gloria Rothstein, illustrations by Lizzy Rockwell. HarperCollins, 2003. Ten little sheep look for ways to stall bedtime.

Sheep Don't Count Sheep by Margaret Wise Brown, illustrations by Benrei Huang. Margaret K. McElderry Books, 2003. A little lamb has trouble falling asleep and wonders what to count.

Sheep Trick or Treat by Nancy Shaw, illustrations by Margot Apple. Houghton Mifflin, 1997. Sheep disguised for Halloween frighten nearby wolves.

Skunks

Carlos and the Skunk by Jan Romero Stevens, illustrations by Jeanne Arnold. Turtleback, 2001. Carlos finds himself in a difficult and hilarious situation when he tries to catch a skunk.

The Dog Who Cried "Woof!" by Bob Barkly, illustrations by John Kurtz. Scholastic, 2001. Based on the Clifford series. Because Cleo had fooled them twice before, Clifford and T-Bone ignore her cries for help.

The Fabulous Four Skunks by David Fair, illustrations by Bruce Koscielniak. Houghton Mifflin, 1996. Four skunks form a rock and roll band, but at their first audition they are told they stink. Nevertheless, the Fabulous Four Skunks are destined for success.

Lizard's Guest by George Shannon, illustrations by Jose Aruego and Ariane Dewey. HarperCollins, 2003. Lizard accidentally steps on Skunk's toe and must pay the consequences.

Magic Matt and the Skunk in the Tub by Grace Maccarone. Scholastic, 2003. When Magic Matt tries to conjure up a rubber duck to play with while he takes a bath, he makes a skunk appear instead.

Skunks! by David Greenberg, illustrations by Lynn Munsinger. Little, Brown and Company, 2001. A comical suggestion of things to do with skunks.

Stinky, My Best Friend: Stinky the Skunk by Everett Uphoff, illustrations by Marcy U. Effinger. Rainbow Artists, 1995. Part of a farm series of moral stories. An orphaned skunk is adopted by a farm boy and his sister.

The Tail of the Skunk by Marsha Diane Arnold, illustrations by Michael Terry. Golden Books, 2002. A Road to Reading book in which Little Skunk worries about how he will escape if Big Bear comes down from the mountains.

Snakes

The Bird, the Monkey and the Snake in the Jungle by Kate Banks, illustrations by Tomasz Bogacki. Farrar, Straus and Giroux, 1999. A rebus story featuring three creatures searching for a new home.

Dance Y'all by Bettye Stroud, illustrations by Van Wright Cornelious and Ying-Hwa Hu. Marshall Cavendish, 2001. With help from relatives, Jack Henry overcomes his fear of the long coachwhip snake he's seen in the barn.

I Need a Snake by Lynne Jonell, illustrations by Petra Mathers. Putnam, 1998. A young boy who wants a pet snake finds an inventive way to have one.

Jag's New Friend by LeAnn Rimes, illustrations by Richard Bernal. Penguin Group, 2004. Feeling neglected by her friends, Jag starts spending time with a snake named Bo, but soon realizes that she has put her friend in danger.

Jimmy's Boa and the Bungee Jump Slam Dunk by Trinka Hakes Noble, illustrations by Steven Kellogg. Penguin Putnam, 2003. Jimmy's boa constrictor creates havoc in his gym class and his antics lead to the formation of an unusual basketball team.

Never Fear, Snake My Dear! by Rolf Siegenthaler. North-South Books, 2001. A caged snake dreams about freedom and going back to his homeland, and a mouse helps him out.

Shawn O'Hisser, the Last Snake in Ireland by Peter J. Welling. Pelican, 2002. "Are there snakes in Ireland?" Shawn O'Hisser can tell you because he unraveled that mystery many years ago. A new twist to an old tale.

Turtle and Snake's Day at the Beach by Kate Spohn. Viking, 2003. Turtle and Snake enter a sand castle contest, but their castle disappears. See also *Turtle and Snake Go Camping* (Viking, 2000).

Verdi by Janell Cannon. Harcourt, 1997. Verdi the snake refuses to turn green when he grows and lands himself into a heap of trouble.

Squirrels

Beaver Gets Lost by Ariane Chottin, illustrations by Marcelle Geneste. Reader's Digest, 2001. A squirrel family takes in a lost beaver and helps him find his family.

Chestnut Dreams by Halina Below. Fitzhenry & Whiteside, 2000. Anya and her grandmother observe the changes in a horse chestnut tree from season to season. Although the book is more about the tree, there are many lively illustrations of squirrels in daily activities.

Heart to Heart by George Shannon, illustrations by Steve Björkman. Houghton Mifflin, 1995. Squirrel tries to make a valentine card for his friend Mole, but discovers a better gift.

Micawber by John Lithgow, illustrations by C. F. Payne. Simon & Schuster, 2002. A squirrel fascinated by art finds a way to create his own masterpieces.

Nuts to You! by Lois Ehlert. Harcourt, 1993. A squirrel has an indoor adventure in a city apartment.

Rosie to the Rescue by Bethany Roberts, illustrations by Kay Chorao. Henry Holt & Company, 2003. As she waits for her parents to return, Rosie the squirrel imagines all sorts of dangers that might befall them.

Squirrel Park by Lisa Campbell Ernst. Bradbury Press, 1993. A boy disagrees with his father over the design of a park that threatens an old oak tree where his squirrel friend lives.

Tomorrow, Up and Away! by Pat Lowery Collins, illustrations by Lynn Munsinger. Houghton Mifflin, 1990. When turtle tells squirrel he'd like to fly, squirrel comes up with an idea.

The Treasure Chest by Dominique Falda. North-South Books, 1999. Squirrel's friends fear he will forget them when he uncovers a treasure chest.

What You Do Is Easy, What I Do Is Hard by Jake Wolf, illustrations by Anna Dewdney. Greenwillow Books, 1996. A self-important squirrel takes over the activities of a bee, an ant, a robin and a spider.

The Wild Woods by Simon James. Candlewick Press, 1993. A Grandfather explains to his grandchild why she can't keep a squirrel for a pet.

Tigers

Close Your Eyes by Kate Banks, illustrations by George Hallensleben. Frances Foster Books, 2002. A mother tiger coaxes her children to sleep by telling them everything they can see with their eyes closed.

"It's Simple," Said Simon by Mary Ann Hoberman, illustrations by Meilo So. Knopf, 2001. After meeting several other animals, Simon meets a tiger that he must outwit before he becomes the tiger's dinner.

Little Tiger's Big Surprise by Julie Sykes, illustrations by Tim Warnes. Little Tiger Press, 1999. Little Tiger isn't sure he wants a baby brother or sister after seeing the new babies in other animals' families. See also *I Don't Want to Take a Bath!* (Little Tiger Press, 1998).

The Rat and the Tiger by Keiko Kasza. Putnam, 1993. Tiger takes advantage of his size with his friend Rat, but Rat stands up for his rights.

Sam and the Tigers: A New Telling of Little Black Sambo by Julius Lester, illustrations by Jerry Pinkney. Dial, 1996. A retelling of the famous story of a little boy who outwits the tigers.

Tiger Baby by Susi Bohdal. North-South Books, 2001. After hearing stories about the white mountains from his mother, Tiger Baby and some friends set out to see them.

Tiger, Tiger by Dee Lillegard, illustrations by Susan Guevara. Putnam, 2002. A boy uses a magic feather to create a tiger, but he must use the feather again to save his village when the tiger gets hungry.

Tiger Trail by Kay Winters, illustrations by Laura Regan. Simon & Schuster, 2000. A mother tiger cares for and teaches her two cubs.

The Tiger Who Lost His Stripes by Anthony Paul, illustrations by Michael Foreman. Harcourt, 1995. When his stripes disappear, General McTiger tries to get them back by outwitting the crafty python who stole them.

Tigress by Helen Cowcher. Farrar, Straus and Giroux, 1991. Herdsmen work with a wildlife sanctuary range to keep their animals safe from a tigress.

Tigress by Nick Dowson, illustrations by Jan Chapman. Candlewick Press, 2004. A mother tigress raises two cubs and teaches them all they need to know until they are ready to rely on themselves.

Who Is the Beast? by Keith Baker. Harcourt, 1990. A tiger is confused by jungle animals running from a beast until he discovers that he is the beast they are running from.

Turtles

Box Turtle at Long Pond by William T. George, illustrations by Lindsay Barrett George. Greenwillow Books, 1989. Describes a typical day for a box turtle at the pond.

Hare and Tortoise Race to the Moon by Oliver J. Corwin. H. N. Abrams, 2002. Best friends Tortoise and Hare compete to see who will be first to reach the moon.

Hi Harry! The Moving Story of How One Slow Tortoise Slowly Made a Friend by Martin Waddell, illustrations by Barbara Firth. Candlewick Press, 2003. Harry has trouble finding a friend as slow as he is.

A Home for Little Turtle by Ariane Chottin, illustrations by Pascale Wirth. Reader's Digest, 2001. A turtle becomes unhappy with her shell.

Hurry and the Monarch by Antoine O'Flatharta, illustrations Meilo So. Random House, 2005. Hurry the tortoise befriends a monarch butterfly when she stops in his garden during migration.

In the Middle of the Puddle by Mike Thaler, illustrations by Bruce Degen. Harper, 1988. A frog and a turtle watch the rain turn their puddle into an ocean.

Mordant's Wish by Valerie Coursen. Henry Holt & Company, 1997. A mole wishes that a turtle-shaped cloud could be his friend.

Tortoise Brings the Mail by Dee Lillegard, illustrations by Jillian Lund. Dutton, 1997. Tortoise is slow delivering the mail and other animals offer to help.

Turtle and Snake's Day at the Beach by Kate Spohn. Viking, 2003. Turtle and Snake enter a sand castle contest, but their castle disappears. See also *Turtle and Snake Go Camping* (Viking, 2000).

Turtle in the Sea by Jim Arnosky. Putnam, 2002. A turtle leaves the sea to lay her eggs in the sand.

Turtle Splash! Countdown at the Pond by Cathryn Falwell. Greenwillow Books, 2001. One by one, ten turtles on a log are startled off by nearby activities.

Turtle Time: A Bedtime Story by Sandol Stoddard, illustrations by Lynn Munsinger. Houghton Mifflin, 1995. A little girl compares herself to her pet turtle while climbing into bed.

What Newt Could Do for Turtle by Jonathan London, illustrations by Louise Voce. Candlewick Press, 1996. A friendship story of a Newt and a Turtle.

When I Grow Up by Peter Horn, illustrations by Kristinah Kadmon. North-South Books, 1999. A little turtle discusses with his father the types of jobs he could do when he grows up.

Whose Hat Is It? by Valeri Gorbachev. HarperCollins, 2004. When someone's hat blows off in the wind, turtle asks various animals if it belongs to one of them.

Making the Puppets

Note: All puppet patterns are located on pages 81–150. You will need to reduce or enlarge all patterns, depending on whether the puppeteer is an adult or a child.

For Most Puppet Patterns You Will Need:

- tape
- glue
- scissors
- needle and thread (to match body felt color) or sewing machine *(optional)*

Making the Bat Puppet

Pattern Pieces and Fabric Needed:

- Pattern piece 1—body (black felt)*
- Pattern piece 2—wing (black felt)*
- 2 outer eyes (yellow felt)
- 2 inner eyes (black felt)
- 2 gleams for the eyes (white felt)
- 2 fangs (white felt)
- nose (pink felt)

* See instructions before cutting.

Other Materials Needed:

- gray fabric paint or marker

Instructions:

1. Copy all paper pattern pieces. Cut two of the wing pattern pieces.

2. Tape the wing patterns in place on the body pattern. (Note that one wing will be turned backwards.)

3. Cut each pattern piece from the appropriate color of felt. Cut two of the joined body piece.

4. Stitch or glue the body pieces together, leaving the bottom open.

5. Glue the outer eyes, inner eyes and gleams in place.

6. Glue the nose in place.

7. Draw the mouth with gray fabric paint or marker.

8. Glue the fangs in place.

Making the Bear Puppet

Pattern Pieces and Fabric Needed:

- Pattern piece 1—upper body (brown felt)*
- Pattern piece 2—lower body (brown felt)*
- 2 outer eyes (white felt)
- 2 inner eyes (black felt)
- 2 gleams for the eyes (white felt)
- nose (pink felt)
- mouth (pink felt)
- inner ears (beige felt)
- muzzle (beige felt)
- tummy (beige felt)
- 6 finger pads (beige felt)

* See instructions before cutting.

Other Materials Needed:

- black fabric paint or marker

Instructions:

1. Copy all paper pattern pieces. Tape the upper body to the lower body along the dotted lines.

2. Cut each pattern piece from the appropriate color of felt. Cut two of the joined body piece.

3. Stitch or glue the body pieces together, leaving the bottom open.

4. Glue the outer eyes, inner eyes and gleams in place. Draw eyebrows with black fabric paint or marker. *(Optional)*

5. Glue the inner ears in place.

6. Glue the muzzle in place.

7. Glue the nose in place.

8. Draw lines for the mouth with black fabric paint or marker.

9. Glue the mouth in place.

10. Glue the tummy in place.

11. Glue the finger pads in place.

Making the Bird Puppet

Pattern Pieces and Fabric Needed:

- Pattern piece 1—upper body (brightly colored felt)

- Pattern piece 2—lower body (brightly colored felt)

- 2 outer eyes (white felt)

- 2 inner eyes (black felt)

- 2 gleams for the eyes (white felt)

- beak (orange felt)

- tail (brightly colored felt)

Instructions:

1. Copy all paper pattern pieces. Tape the upper body to the lower body along the dotted lines.

2. Cut each pattern piece from the appropriate color of felt. Cut two of the joined body piece.

3. Stitch or glue the body pieces together, leaving the bottom open.

4. Glue the outer eyes, inner eyes and gleams in place.

5. Glue the beak in place.

6. Glue the tail in place.

Making the Cat Puppet

Pattern Pieces and Fabric Needed:

- Pattern piece 1—upper body (light gray felt)*

- Pattern piece 2—lower body (light gray felt)*

- 2 outer eyes (white felt)

- 2 inner eyes (green felt)

- 2 gleams for the eyes (white felt)

- nose (pink felt)

- tongue (pink felt)

- inner ears (pink felt)

- tummy (pink felt)

- 6 finger pads (pink felt)

- tail (light gray felt)

* See instructions before cutting.

Other Materials Needed:

- black fabric paint or marker

Instructions:

1. Copy all required paper pattern pieces. Tape the upper body to the lower body along the dotted lines.

2. Cut each pattern piece from the appropriate color of felt. Cut two of the joined body piece.

3. Stitch or glue the body pieces together, leaving the bottom open.

4. Glue the outer eyes, inner eyes and gleams in place.

5. Glue the inner ears in place.

6. Glue the nose in place.

7. Draw lines for the mouth with black fabric paint or marker.

8. Glue the tongue in place.

9. Draw whiskers with black fabric paint or marker.

10. Glue the tummy in place.

11. Glue the finger pads in place.

12. Glue the tail in place.

Making the Chicken Puppet

Pattern Pieces and Fabric Needed:

- Pattern piece 1—body (beige felt)
- 2 outer eyes (white felt)
- 2 inner eyes (black felt)
- 2 gleams for the eyes (white felt)
- tail (red felt)
- wing (red felt)
- comb (red felt)
- wattle (red felt)
- beak (yellow felt)

Other Materials Needed:

- black fabric paint or marker (optional)

Instructions:

1. Copy all required paper pattern pieces.

2. Cut each pattern piece from the appropriate color of felt. Cut two of the body.

3. Stitch or glue the body pieces together, leaving the bottom open.

4. Glue the outer eyes, inner eyes and gleams in the eyes in place. Draw eyebrows with black fabric paint or marker (optional).

5. Glue the wing in place.

6. Glue the tail in place.

7. Glue the beak in place.

8. Glue the wattle in place.

9. Glue the comb in place.

Making the Cow Puppet

Pattern Pieces and Fabric Needed:

- Pattern piece 1—upper body (white felt)
- Pattern piece 2—lower body (white felt)
- tail (white felt)
- 2 outer eyes (white felt)
- 2 inner eyes (black felt)
- 2 gleams for the eyes (white felt)
- snout (pink felt)
- 2 nostrils (black felt)
- hooves (brown felt)
- 2 horns (brown felt)
- horn brace (golden brown felt)
- spots (black felt)

Other Materials Needed:

- black fabric paint or marker

Instructions:

1. Copy all paper pattern pieces. Tape the upper body to the lower body along the dotted lines.

2. Cut each pattern piece from the appropriate color of felt. Cut two of the joined body piece.

3. Stitch or sew the horn pattern piece together. Leave no opening.

4. Glue the horn brace onto the horn.

5. Fit the horn between the body pattern pieces.

6. Stitch or sew the body pieces together, leaving the bottom open.

7. Glue the outer eyes, inner eyes and gleams in place.

8. Glue the snout in place.

9. Glue the nostrils in place.

10. Draw the line for the mouth with black fabric paint or marker.

11. Glue the hooves in place.

12. Glue the spots in place.

13. Glue the tail in place.

Making the Crocodile/ Alligator Puppet

Pattern Pieces and Fabric Needed:

- Pattern piece 1—upper body (green felt)

- Pattern piece 2—lower body (green felt)

- tail (green felt)

- 2 outer eyes (yellow felt)

- 2 inner eyes (black felt)

- 2 gleams for the eyes (white felt)

- snout (green felt)

- 2 nostrils (black felt)

- 6 claws (white felt)

- teeth (white felt)

Other Materials Needed:

- black fabric paint or marker

Instructions:

1. Copy all paper pattern pieces. Tape the upper body to the lower body along the dotted lines.

2. Cut each pattern piece from the appropriate color of felt. Cut two of the joined body piece.

3. Stitch or sew the body pieces together, leaving the bottom open.

4. Glue the outer eyes, inner eyes and gleams in place.

5. Draw eyebrows with black fabric paint or marker. *(Optional)*

6. Glue the snout in place.

7. Glue the nostrils in place.

8. Draw the line for the mouth with black fabric paint or marker.

9. Glue the teeth in place.

10. Glue the claws in place.

11. Glue the tail in place.

Making the Dog Puppet

Pattern Pieces and Fabric Needed:

- Pattern piece 1—upper body (brown felt)

- Pattern piece 2—lower body (brown felt)

- tail (brown felt)

- 6 finger pads (beige felt)

- 2 outer eyes (white felt)

- 2 inner eyes (black felt)

- 2 gleams for the eyes (white felt)

- 2 ears (dark brown felt)
- tummy (beige felt)
- nose (black felt)
- tongue (pink felt)

Other Materials Needed:

- black fabric paint or marker

Instructions:

1. Copy all paper pattern pieces. Tape the upper body to the lower body along the dotted lines.

2. Cut each pattern piece from the appropriate color of felt. Cut two of the joined body piece.

3. Stitch or sew the body pieces together, leaving the bottom open.

4. Glue the outer eyes, inner eyes and gleams in place.

5. Glue the nose in place.

6. Draw the line for the mouth with black fabric paint or marker. Draw freckles with black fabric paint or marker.

7. Glue the tongue in place.

8. Glue the ears in place.

9. Glue the tummy in place.

10. Glue the finger pads in place.

11. Glue the tail in place.

Making the Duck Puppet

Pattern Pieces and Fabric Needed:

- Pattern piece 1—upper body (yellow felt)
- Pattern piece 2—lower body (yellow felt)
- tail (yellow felt)
- 2 outer eyes (white felt)
- 2 inner eyes (black felt)

- 2 gleams for the eyes (white felt)
- bill (orange felt)

Other Materials Needed:

- black fabric paint or marker

Instructions:

1. Copy all paper pattern pieces. Tape the upper body to the lower body along the dotted lines.

2. Cut each pattern piece from the appropriate color of felt. Cut two of the joined body piece.

3. Stitch or sew the body pieces together, leaving the bottom open.

4. Glue the outer eyes, inner eyes and gleams in place.

5. Glue the bill in place.

6. Draw the nostrils with black fabric paint or marker.

7. Glue the tail in place.

Making the Elephant Puppet

Pattern Pieces and Fabric Needed:

- Pattern piece 1—upper body (gray felt)
- Pattern piece 2—lower body (gray felt)
- trunk (gray felt)
- ears (gray felt)
- 2 outer eyes (white felt)
- 2 inner eyes (black felt)
- 2 gleams for the eyes (white felt)
- inner ears (black felt) *(optional)*

Other Materials Needed:

- black fabric paint or marker

Instructions:

1. Copy all paper pattern pieces. Tape the upper body to the lower body along dotted lines.

2. Cut each pattern piece from the appropriate color of felt. Cut two of the joined body piece.

3. Stitch or sew the body pieces together, leaving the bottom open.

4. Glue the outer eyes, inner eyes and gleams in place.

5. Glue the trunk in place.

6. Glue the ears in place.

7. Glue the inner ears in place. (Optional)

8. Draw lines over the trunk and on the forehead with black fabric paint or marker.

Making the Fish Puppet

Pattern Pieces and Fabric Needed:

- Pattern piece 1— body front (gray felt)

- Pattern piece 2— body back (gray felt)

- 2 outer eyes (white felt)

- 2 inner eyes (black felt)

Other Materials Needed:

- metallic gray or silver fabric paint or marker

Instructions:

1 Copy all paper pattern pieces. Tape the body front to the body back along dotted lines.

2. Cut each pattern piece from the appropriate color of felt. Cut two of the joined body piece.

3. Stitch or sew the body pieces together, leaving the bottom open.

4. Glue the outer eyes and inner eyes in place.

5. Draw lines on the fin and tail with metallic gray or silver fabric paint or marker.

Making the Frog Puppet

Pattern Pieces Needed:

- Pattern piece 1—upper body (green felt)

- Pattern piece 2—lower body (green felt)

- 2 outer eyes (yellow felt)

- 2 inner eyes (black felt)

- 2 gleams for the eyes (white felt)

- 2 eyelids (green felt)

- nostrils (black felt)

- tongue (red felt)

- 6 finger circles (lime green felt)

- spots (lime green felt)

Other Materials Needed:

- black fabric paint or marker

Instructions:

1. Copy all paper pattern pieces. Tape the upper body to the lower body along the dotted lines.

2. Cut each pattern piece from the appropriate color of felt. Cut two of the joined body piece.

3. Stitch or sew the body pieces together, leaving the bottom open.

4. Glue the outer eyes, inner eyes and gleams in place.

5. Glue the eyelid over the top of the eye.

6. Glue the nostrils in place.

7. Draw a line for the mouth with black fabric paint or marker.

8. Glue the tongue in place.

9. Glue the finger circles in place.

10. Glue the spots in place.

Making the Hippopotamus Puppet

Pattern Pieces and Fabric Needed:

- Pattern piece 1—upper body (gray felt)
- Pattern piece 2—lower body (gray felt)
- 2 outer eyes (white felt)
- 2 inner eyes (black felt)
- 2 gleams for the eyes (white felt)
- snout (white felt)
- nostrils
- mouth (gray or pink felt)
- inner ears (pink felt)

Instructions:

1. Copy all paper pattern pieces. Tape the upper body to the lower body along the dotted lines.

2. Cut each pattern piece from the appropriate color of felt. Cut two of the joined body piece.

3. Stitch or sew the body pieces together, leaving the bottom open.

4. Glue the outer eyes, inner eyes and gleams in place.

5. Glue the mouth in place.

6. Glue the snout in place, overlapping the mouth.

7. Glue the nostrils in place.

8. Glue the inner ears in place.

Making the Mouse Puppet

Pattern Pieces and Fabric Needed:

- Pattern piece 1—upper body (gray felt)
- Pattern piece 2—lower body (gray felt)
- tail (gray felt)
- 2 outer eyes (white felt)
- 2 inner eyes (black felt)
- 2 gleams for the eyes (white felt)
- nose (pink felt)
- teeth (white felt)
- inner ears (pink felt)
- 6 finger pads (pale gray felt)
- tummy (pale gray felt)

Other Materials Needed:

- black fabric paint or marker

Instructions:

1. Copy all paper pattern pieces. Tape the upper body to the lower body along the dotted lines.

2. Cut each pattern piece from the appropriate color of felt. Cut two of the joined body piece.

3. Stitch or sew the body pieces together, leaving the bottom open.

4. Glue the outer eyes, inner eyes and gleams in place.

5. Draw eyelashes with black fabric paint or marker. *(Optional)*

6. Glue the nose in place.

7. Draw a line for the mouth with black fabric paint or marker.

8. Draw whiskers with black fabric paint or marker. *(Optional)*

9. Glue the teeth in place.

10. Glue the inner ears in place.

11. Glue the tummy in place.

12. Glue the finger pads in place.

13. Glue the tail in place.

Making the Monkey Puppet

Pattern Pieces and Fabric Needed:

- Pattern piece 1—upper body (brown felt)

- Pattern piece 2—lower body (brown felt)
- tail (brown felt)
- 2 outer eyes (white felt)
- 2 inner eyes (black felt)
- 2 gleams for the eyes (white felt)
- face (peach felt)
- tongue (pink felt)
- tummy (peach felt)

Other Materials Needed:

- black fabric paint or marker

Instructions:

1. Copy all paper pattern pieces. Tape the upper body to the lower body along the dotted lines.
2. Cut each pattern piece from the appropriate color of felt. Cut two of the joined body piece.
3. Stitch or sew the body pieces together, leaving the bottom open.
4. Glue the face in place.
5. Glue the outer eyes, inner eyes and gleams in place.
6. Draw a line for the mouth and nose with black fabric paint or marker.
7. Glue the tongue in place.
8. Glue the tummy in place.
9. Glue the tail in place.

Making the Owl Puppet

Pattern Pieces and Fabric Needed:

- Pattern piece 1—upper body (brown felt)
- Pattern piece 2—lower body (brown felt)
- 2 outer eyes (yellow felt)
- 2 inner eyes (black felt)

- 2 gleams for the eyes (white felt)
- beak (yellow felt)
- face (pale brown felt)
- tummy (pale brown felt)

Other Materials Needed:

- black fabric paint or marker

Instructions:

1. Copy all paper pattern pieces. Tape the upper body to the lower body along the dotted lines.
2. Cut each pattern piece from the appropriate color of felt. Cut two of the joined body piece.
3. Stitch or sew the body pieces together, leaving the bottom open.
4. Glue the face in place.
5. Glue the outer eyes, inner eyes and gleams in place.
6. Glue the beak in place.
7. Glue the tummy in place.
8. Draw a line for the ears with black fabric paint or marker.

Making the Pig Puppet

Pattern Pieces and Fabric Needed:

- Pattern piece 1—upper body (pink felt)
- Pattern piece 2—lower body (pink felt)
- 2 outer eyes (white felt)
- 2 inner eyes (black felt)
- 2 gleams for the eyes (white felt)
- snout (pink felt)
- 2 nostrils (black felt)
- mouth (red felt)
- hooves (brown felt)

Other Materials Needed:

- black fabric paint or marker
- pink pipe cleaner, curled around pencil (for tail)

Instructions:

1. Copy all paper pattern pieces. Tape the upper body to the lower body along the dotted lines.

2. Cut each pattern piece from the appropriate color of felt. Cut two of each joined body piece.

3. Stitch or sew the body pieces together, leaving the bottom open.

4. Glue the outer eyes, inner eyes and gleams in the eyes in place.

5. Glue the snout in place.

6. Glue the nostrils in place.

7. Draw a line for the mouth with black fabric paint or marker.

8. Glue the mouth in place.

9. Glue the hooves in place.

10. Attach a curled pipe cleaner for the tail.

Making the Rabbit Puppet

Pattern Pieces and Fabric Needed:

- Pattern piece 1—head (white felt)
- Pattern piece 2—body (white felt)
- 2 outer eyes (pink felt)
- 2 inner eyes (black felt)
- 2 gleams for the eyes (white felt)
- inner ears (pink felt)
- nose (pink felt)
- teeth (white felt)
- 6 finger pads (pink felt)
- tummy (pink felt)

Other Materials Needed:

- black fabric paint or marker
- large white pom-pom (for tail)

Instructions:

1. Copy all paper pattern pieces. Tape the head to the body along dotted lines.

2. Cut each pattern piece from the appropriate color of felt. Cut two of the joined body piece.

3. Stitch or sew the body pieces together, leaving the bottom open.

4. Glue the outer eyes, inner eyes and gleams in place.

5. Glue the nose in place.

6. Draw a line for the mouth with black fabric paint or marker.

7. Glue the teeth in place.

8. Glue the inner ears in place.

9. Glue the tummy in place.

10. Glue the finger pads in place.

11. Glue the pom-pom in place for the tail.

Making the Raccoon Puppet

Pattern Pieces and Fabric Needed:

- Pattern piece 1—upper body (light brown felt)
- Pattern piece 2—lower body (light brown felt)
- tail (light brown felt)
- 2 outer eyes (white felt)
- 2 inner eyes (black felt)
- 2 gleams for the eyes (white felt)
- muzzle (white felt)
- mouth (light brown felt)
- nose (black felt)
- inner ears (black felt)
- brow (white felt)

- eye circles (black felt)

Instructions:

1. Copy all paper pattern pieces. Tape the upper body to the lower body along the dotted lines.

2. Cut each pattern piece from the appropriate color of felt. Cut two of the joined body piece.

3. Stitch or sew the body pieces together, leaving the bottom open.

4. Glue the eye circles in place.

5. Glue the outer eyes, inner eyes and gleams in place.

6. Glue the mouth in place.

7. Glue the muzzle in place, overlapping the mouth.

8. Glue the nose in place.

9. Glue the brow in place.

10. Glue the inner ears in place.

11. Cut stripes of black fabric and glue them to the tail. Trim the edges.

12. Glue the tail in place.

Making the Sheep Puppet

Pattern Pieces and Fabric Needed:

- Pattern piece 1—upper body (dark gray felt)
- Pattern piece 2—lower body (dark gray felt)
- head top (dark gray felt)
- ears (dark gray felt)
- muzzle (light gray felt)
- lip (pink or light gray felt)
- inner ears (pink felt)
- 2 eyelids (light gray felt)
- 2 hooves (black felt)

Other Materials Needed:

- black fabric paint or marker

Instructions:

1. Copy all paper pattern pieces. Tape the upper body to the lower body along the dotted lines.

2. Cut each pattern piece from the appropriate color of felt. Cut two of the joined body piece.

3. Stitch or sew the body pieces together, leaving the bottom open.

4. Glue the eyelids in place.

5. Draw on the eyelashes with black fabric paint or marker.

6. Glue the lip in place.

7. Glue the muzzle in place, slightly overlapping the lip.

8. Draw the nostrils with black fabric paint or marker.

9. Glue the hooves in place.

10. Glue the head top in place.

11. Glue the ears in place.

12. Glue the inner ears in place.

Making the Skunk Puppet

Pattern Pieces and Fabric Needed:

- Pattern piece 1—upper body (black felt)
- Pattern piece 2—lower body (black felt))
- tail (black felt)
- tail stripe (white felt)
- head stripe (white felt)
- 2 outer eyes (white felt)
- 2 inner eyes (black felt)
- 2 gleams for the eyes (white felt)
- nose (pink felt)
- 6 finger pads (pink felt)
- tummy (white felt)

Other Materials Needed:

- black fabric paint or marker

Instructions:

1. Copy all paper pattern pieces. Tape the upper body to the lower body along the dotted lines.

2. Cut each pattern piece from the appropriate color of felt. Cut two of the joined body piece.

3. Stitch or sew the body pieces together, leaving the bottom open.

4. Glue the outer eyes, inner eyes and gleams in place.

5. Glue the nose in place.

6. Draw a line for the mouth with black fabric paint or marker.

7. Glue the tummy in place.

8. Glue the finger pads in place.

9. Glue the head stripe in place.

10. Glue the tail stripe to the tail.

11. Glue the tail in place.

Making the Snake Puppet

Pattern Pieces and Fabric Needed:

- Pattern piece 1—head (green felt)
- Pattern piece 2—body (green felt)
- 2 outer eyes (yellow felt)
- 2 inner eyes (black felt)
- 2 gleams for the eyes (white felt)
- mouth (black felt)
- nostrils (black felt)
- tongue (red felt)
- 2 fangs (white felt)
- 4–8 diamond shapes (lime green felt)

Instructions:

1. Copy all paper pattern pieces. Tape the head to the body along the dotted lines.

---

2. Cut each pattern piece from the appropriate color of felt. Cut two of the joined body piece.

3. Stitch or sew the body pieces together, leaving the bottom open.

4. Glue the outer eyes, inner eyes and gleams in place.

5. Glue the mouth in place.

6. Glue the tongue in place.

7. Glue the fangs in place.

8. Glue the nostrils in place.

9. Glue the diamond shapes onto the snake.

Making the Squirrel Puppet

Pattern Pieces and Fabric Needed:

- Pattern piece 1—upper body (gray felt)
- Pattern piece 2—lower body (gray felt)
- tail (gray felt)
- 2 outer eyes (white felt)
- 2 inner eyes (black felt)
- 2 gleams for the eyes (white felt)
- nose (black felt)
- face (pale gray felt)
- 2 inner ears (pink felt)
- 2 teeth (white felt)

Other Materials Needed:

- black fabric paint or marker

Instructions:

1. Copy all paper pattern pieces. Tape the upper body to the lower body along the dotted lines.

2. Cut each pattern piece from the appropriate color of felt. Cut two of the joined body piece.

3. Stitch or sew the body pieces together, leaving the bottom open.

4. Glue the face in place.

5. Glue the outer eyes, inner eyes and gleams in place.

6. Glue the nose in place.

7. Draw a line for the mouth with black fabric paint or marker.

8. Glue the teeth in place.

9. Glue the inner ears in place.

10. Glue the tail in place.

Making the Tiger Puppet

Pattern Pieces and Fabric Needed:

- Pattern piece 1—upper body (orange felt)

- Pattern piece 2—lower body (orange felt)

- tail (orange felt)

- 2 outer eyes (yellow felt)

- 2 inner eyes (black felt)

- 2 gleams for the eyes (white felt)

- nose (black felt)

- inner ears (cream felt)

- 5 tail stripes (black felt)

- stripes (black felt)

Other Materials Needed:

- black fabric paint or marker

Instructions:

1. Copy all paper pattern pieces. Tape the upper body to the lower body along the dotted lines.

2. Cut each pattern piece from the appropriate color of felt. Cut two of the joined body piece.

3. Stitch or sew the body pieces together, leaving the bottom open.

4. Glue the outer eyes, inner eyes and gleams in place.

5. Glue the nose in place.

6. Draw a line for the mouth with black fabric paint or marker.

7. Glue the inner ears in place.

8. Glue the stripes in place.

9. Glue the tail in place.

10. Glue the tail stripes in place.

Making the Turtle Puppet

Pattern Pieces Needed:

- Pattern piece 1— body front (green felt)

- Pattern piece 2— body back (green felt)

- outer eye (white felt)

- inner eye (black felt)

- gleam for the eye (white felt)

- shell (dark green felt)

Other Materials Needed:

- light green fabric paint or marker

Instructions:

1. Copy all paper pattern pieces. Tape the body front to the body back along the dotted lines.

2. Cut each pattern piece from the appropriate color of felt. Cut two of the body piece.

3. Stitch or sew the body pieces together, leaving an opening between the legs.

4. Glue the outer eye, inner eye and gleam in place.

5. Glue the shell in place.

6. Decorate the shell with light green fabric paint or marker.

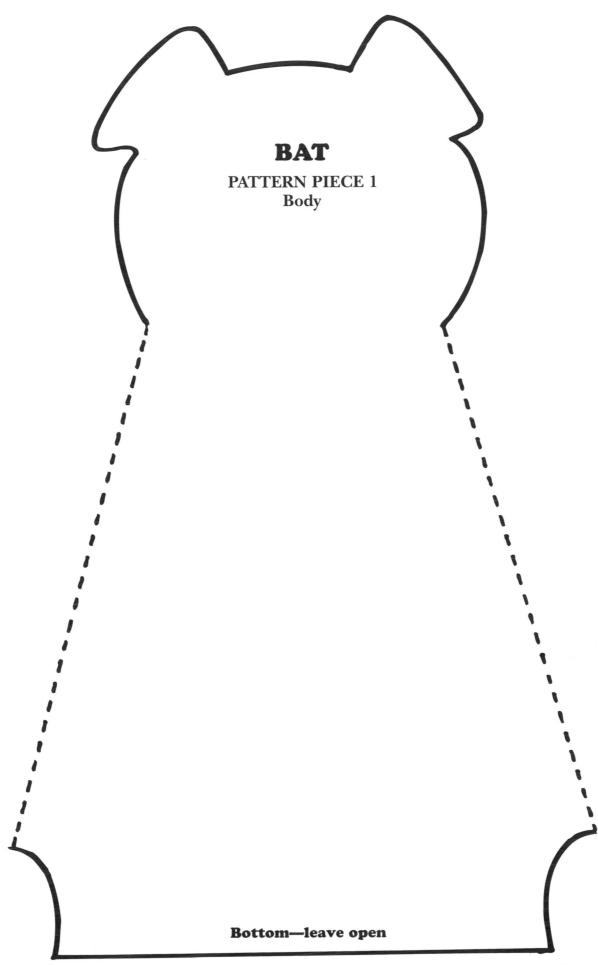

BAT

PATTERN PIECE 1
Body

Bottom—leave open

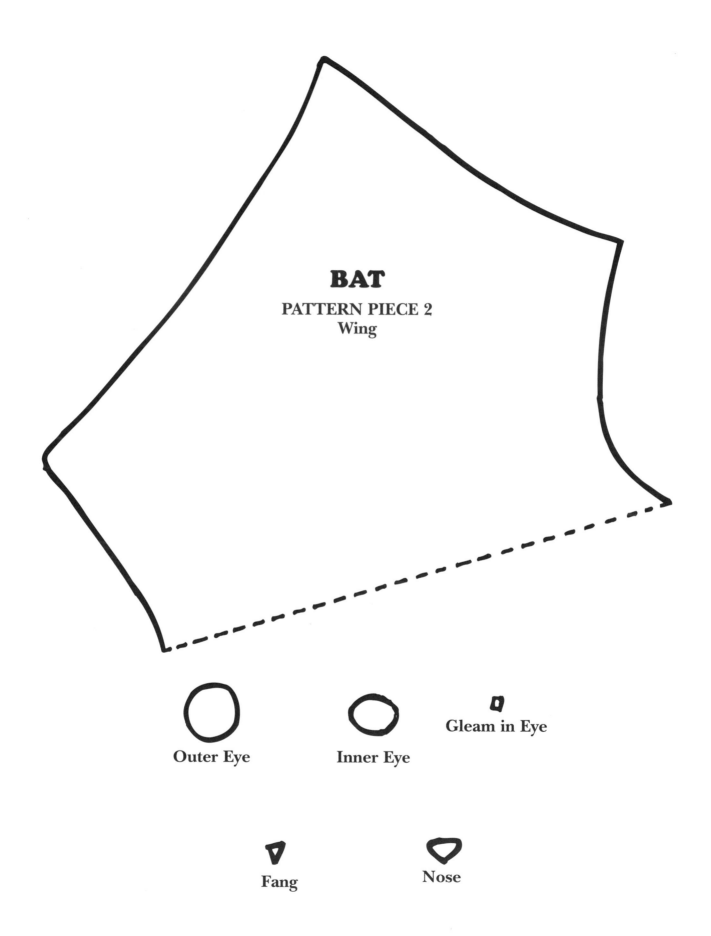

BAT

PATTERN PIECE 2
Wing

Outer Eye

Inner Eye

Gleam in Eye

Fang

Nose

BEAR

PATTERN PIECE 1
Upper Body

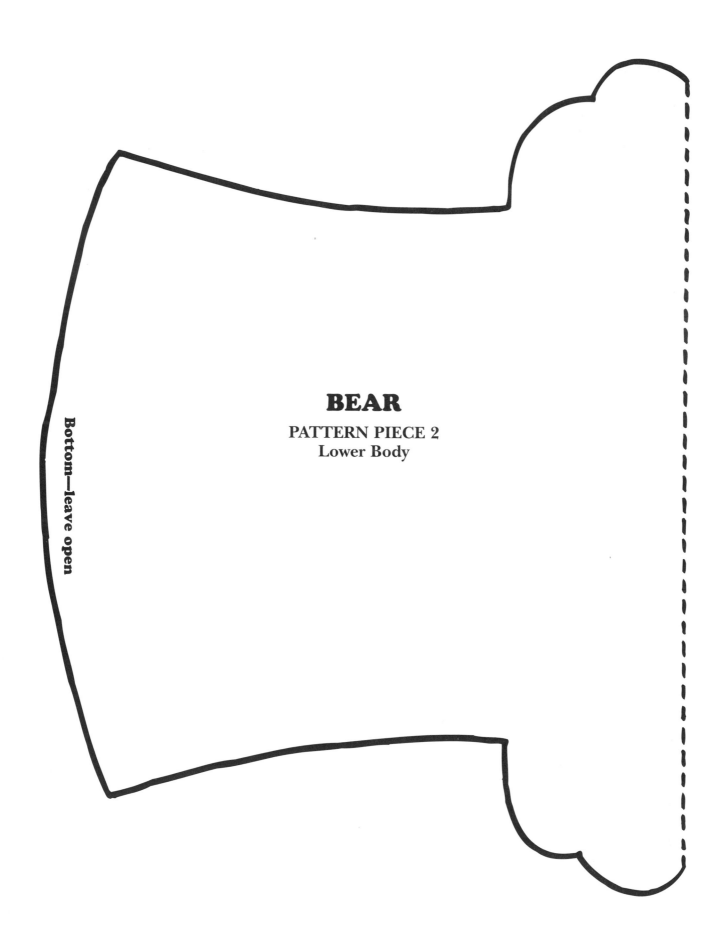

BEAR

PATTERN PIECE 2
Lower Body

Bottom—leave open

BEAR

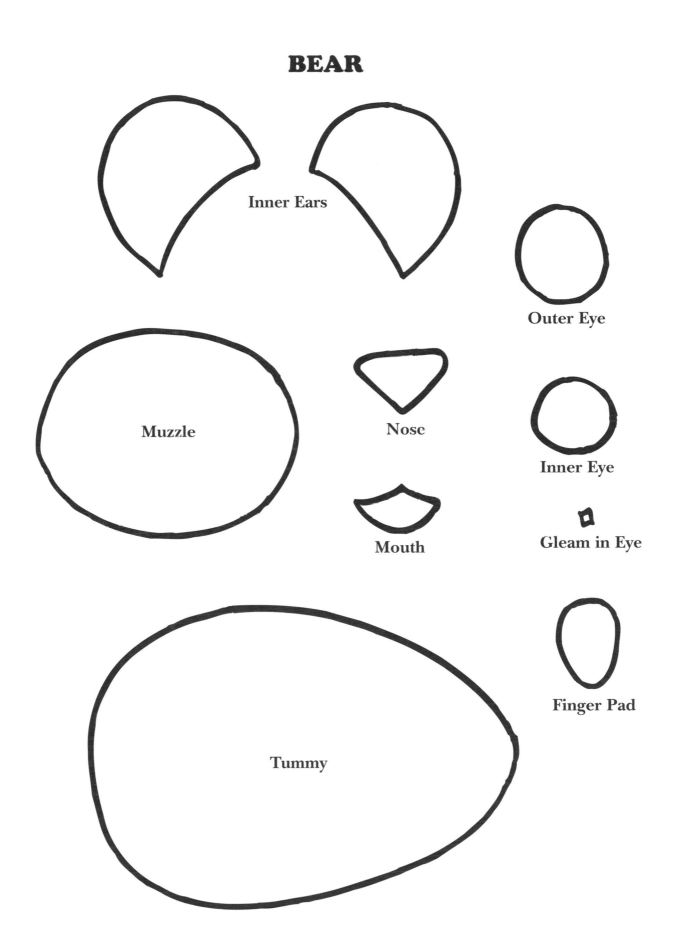

Inner Ears

Outer Eye

Muzzle

Nose

Inner Eye

Mouth

Gleam in Eye

Finger Pad

Tummy

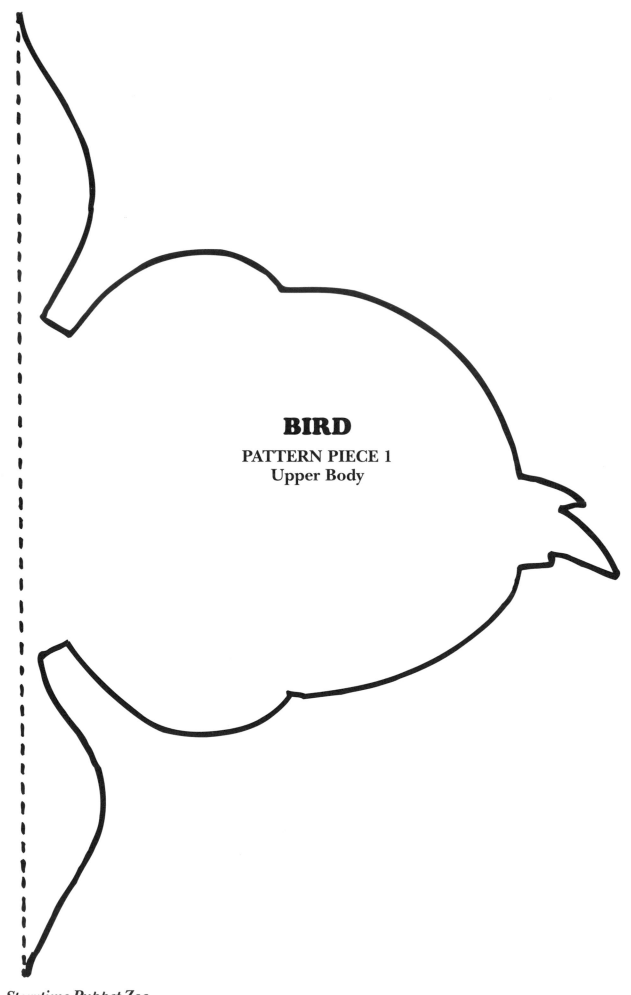

BIRD

PATTERN PIECE 1
Upper Body

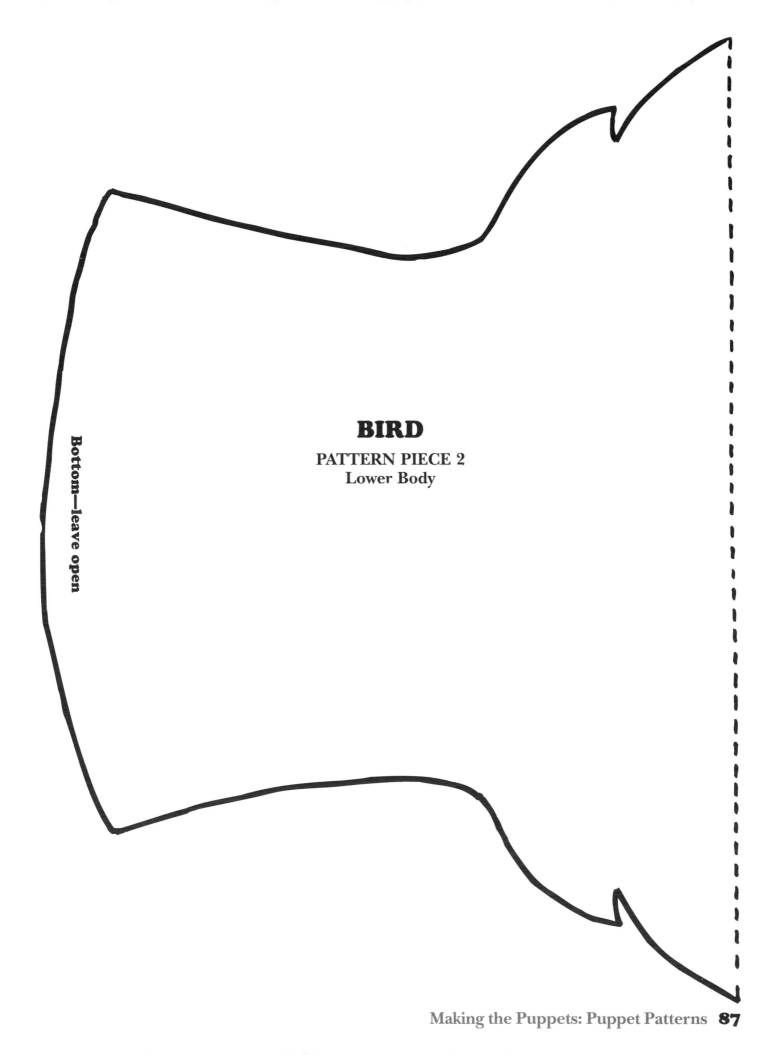

BIRD

PATTERN PIECE 2
Lower Body

Bottom—leave open

BIRD

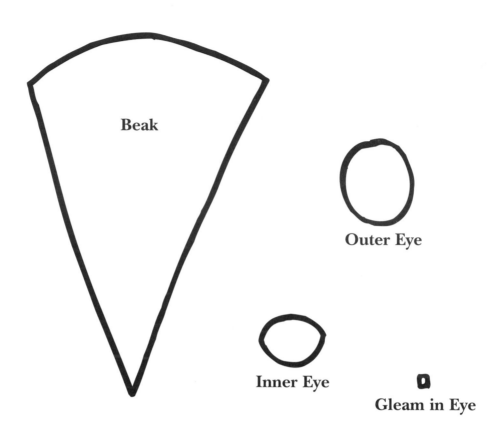

Beak

Outer Eye

Inner Eye

Gleam in Eye

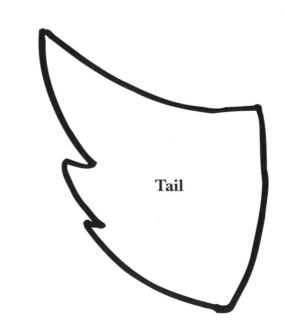

Tail

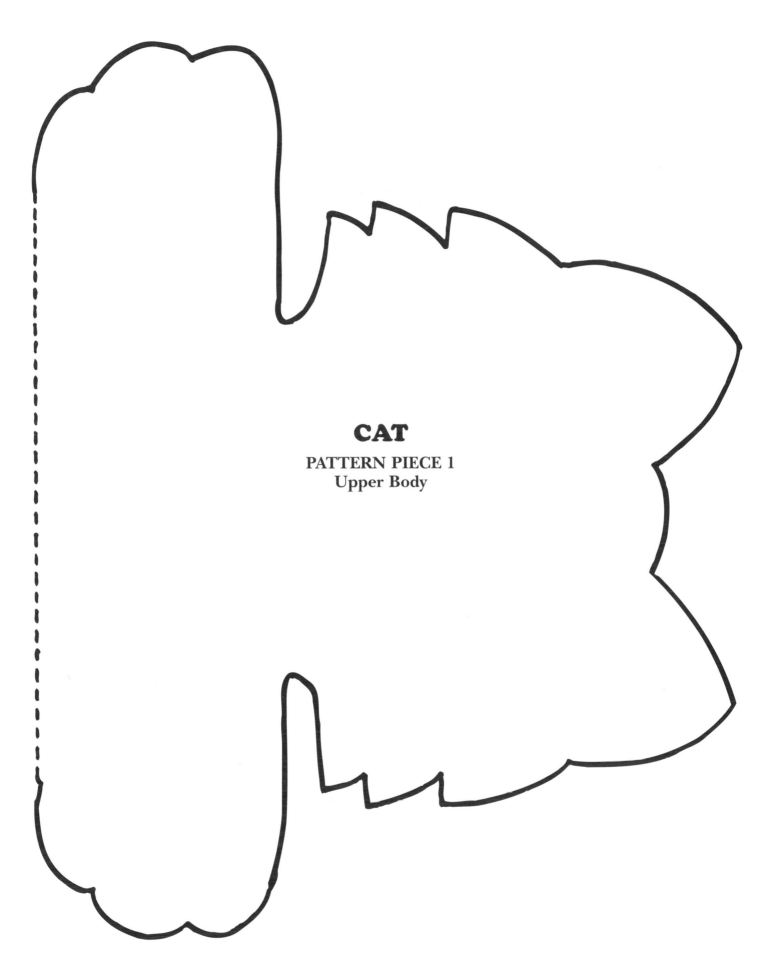

CAT

PATTERN PIECE 1
Upper Body

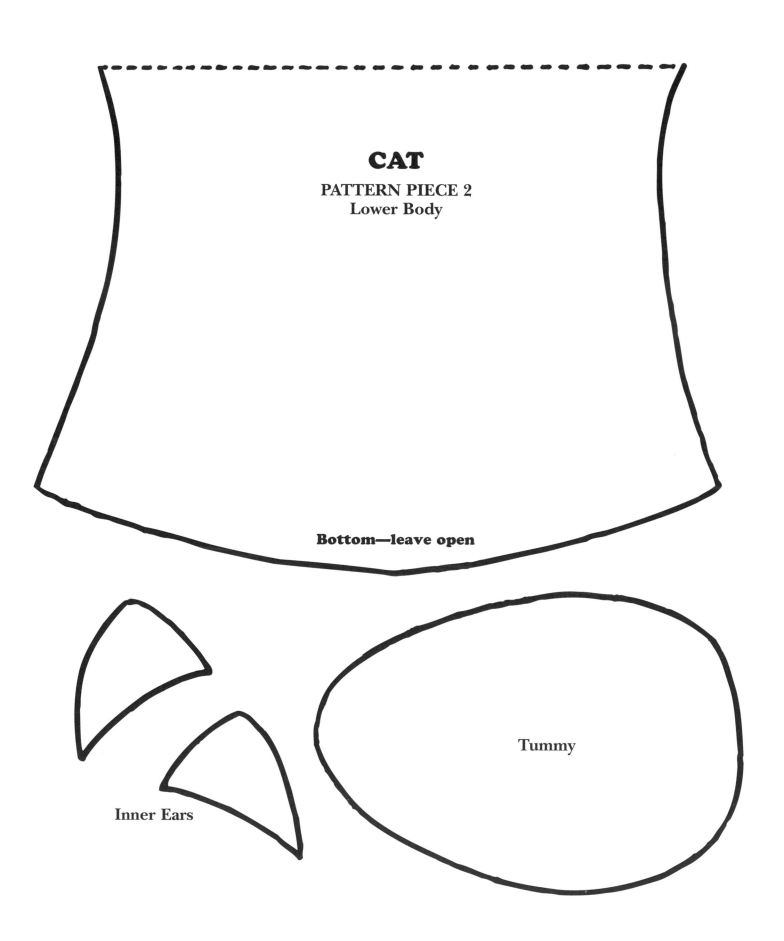

CAT

PATTERN PIECE 2
Lower Body

Bottom—leave open

Inner Ears

Tummy

CAT

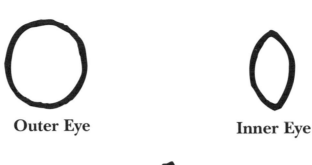

Outer Eye

Inner Eye

Gleam in Eye

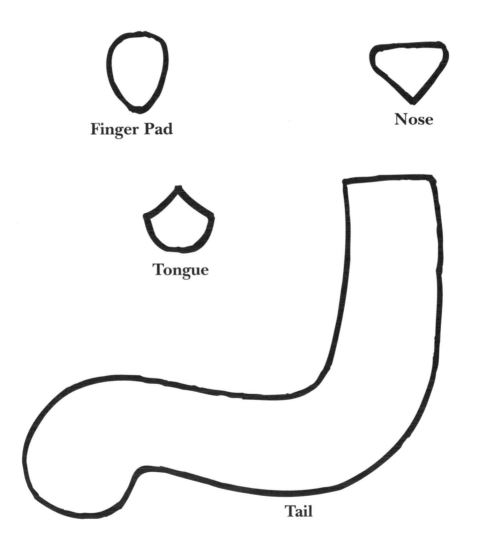

Finger Pad

Nose

Tongue

Tail

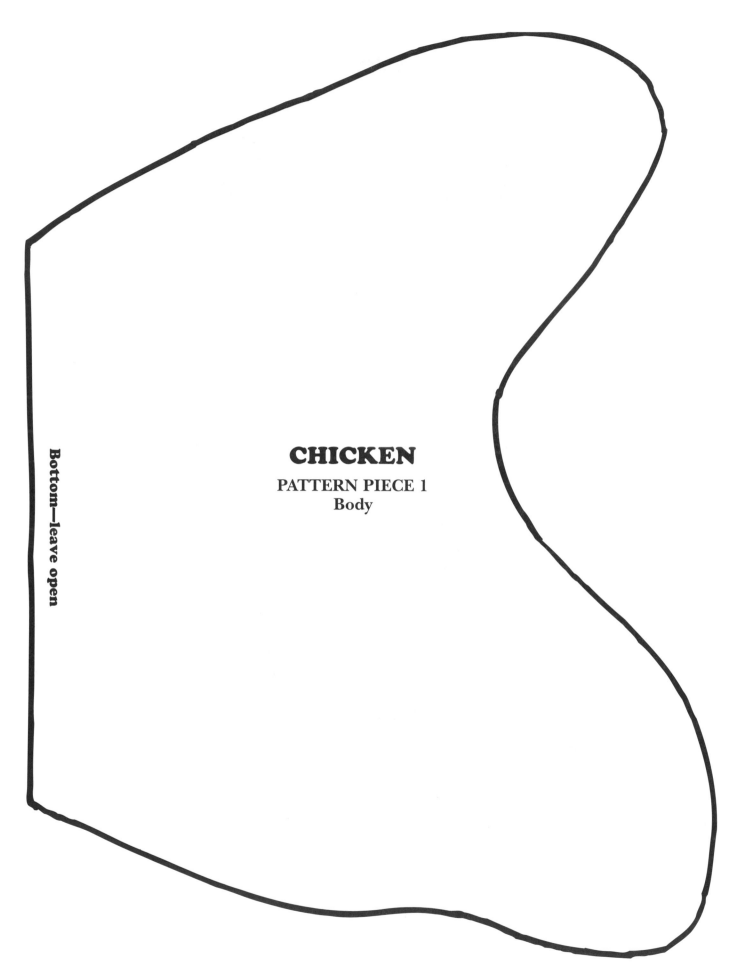

Bottom—leave open

CHICKEN

PATTERN PIECE 1
Body

CHICKEN

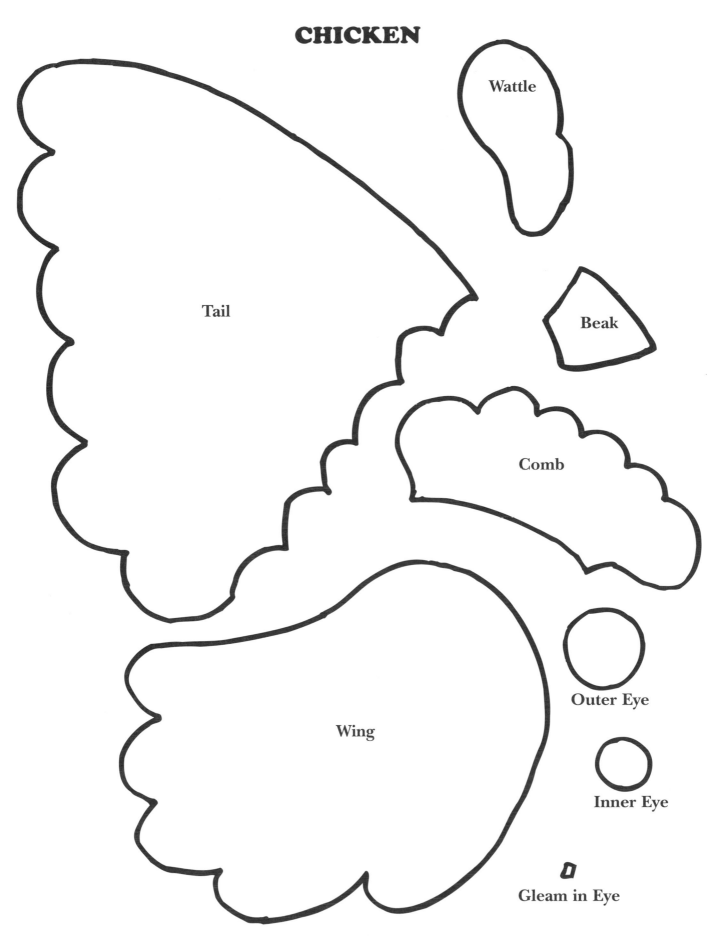

Wattle

Tail

Beak

Comb

Wing

Outer Eye

Inner Eye

Gleam in Eye

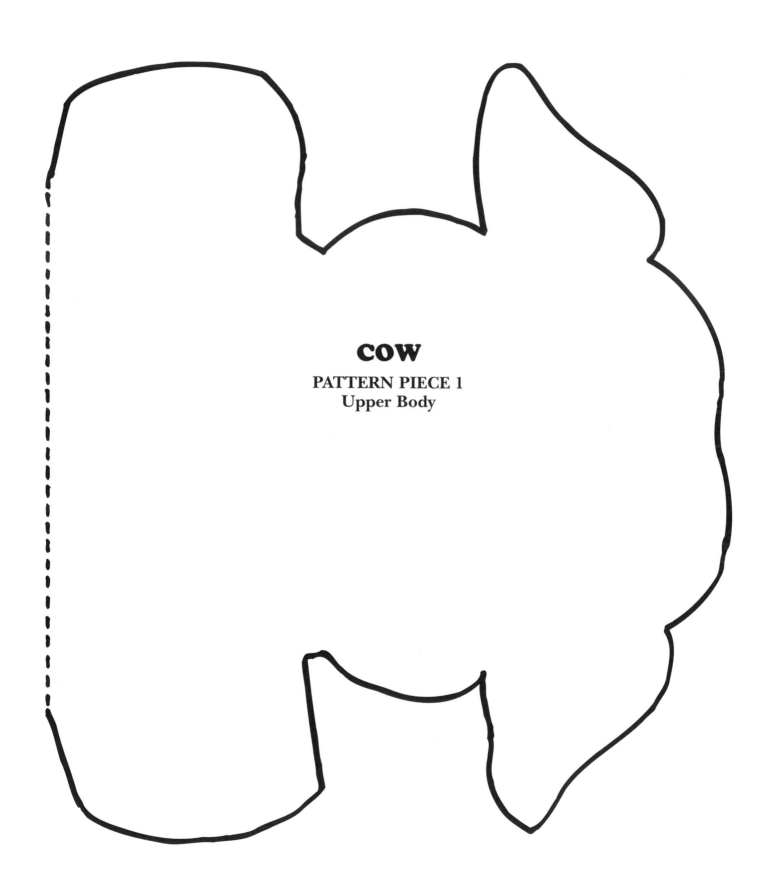

COW
PATTERN PIECE 1
Upper Body

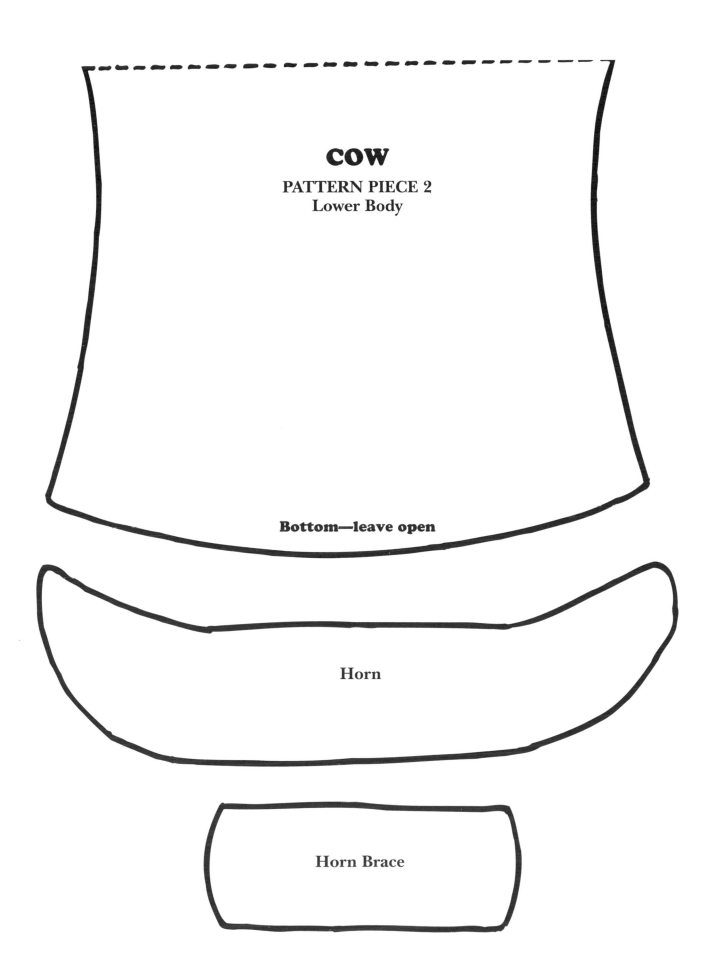

COW

PATTERN PIECE 2
Lower Body

Bottom—leave open

Horn

Horn Brace

COW

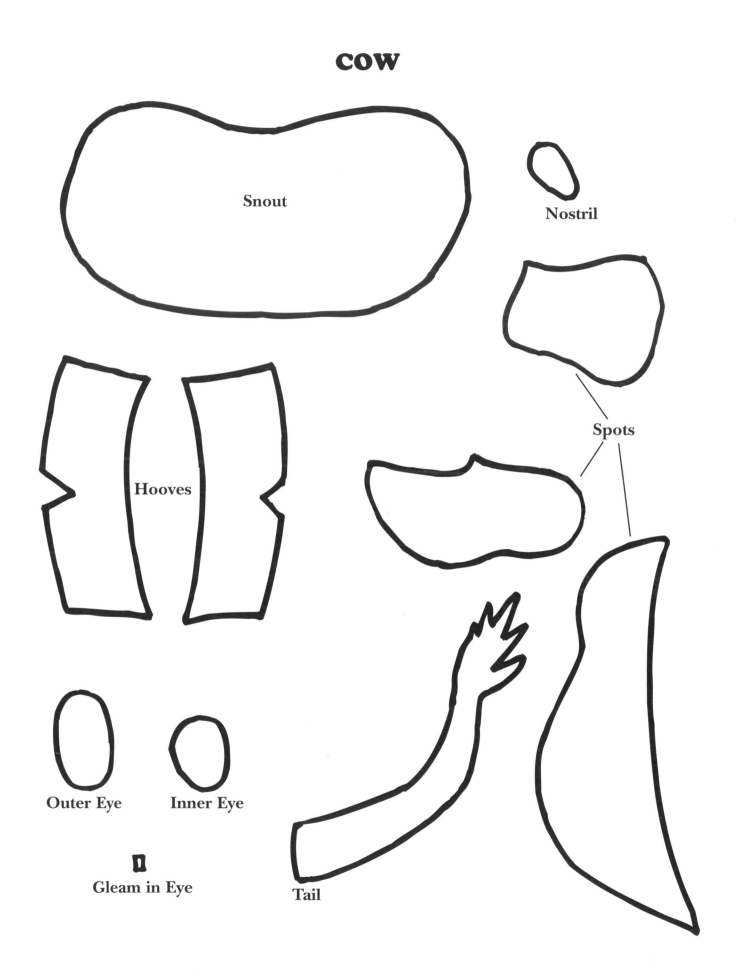

Snout

Nostril

Spots

Hooves

Outer Eye

Inner Eye

Gleam in Eye

Tail

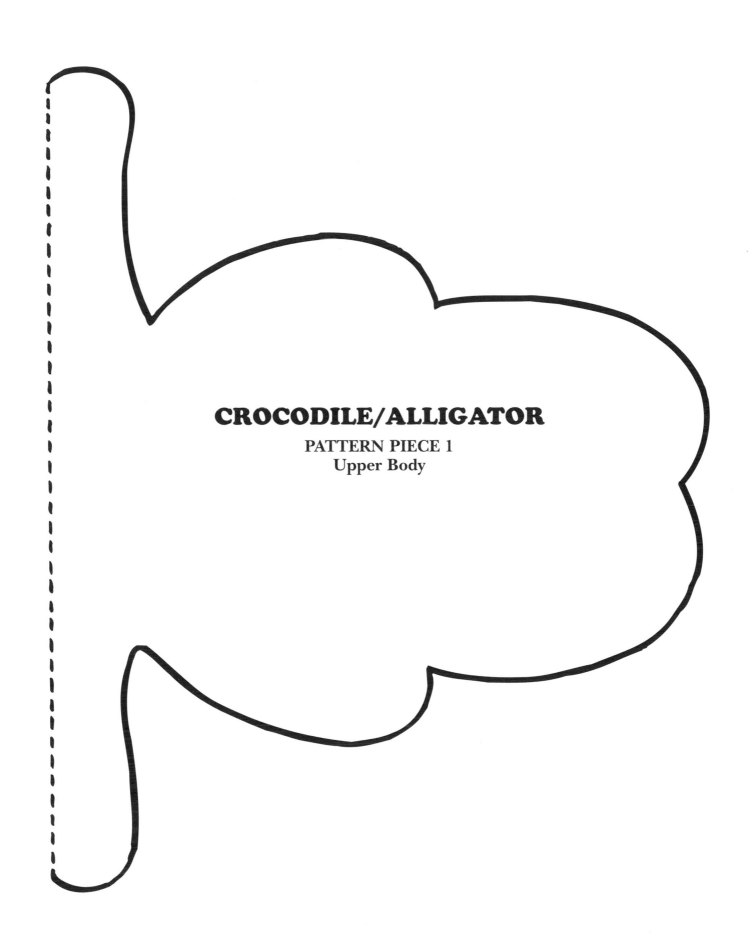

CROCODILE/ALLIGATOR

PATTERN PIECE 1
Upper Body

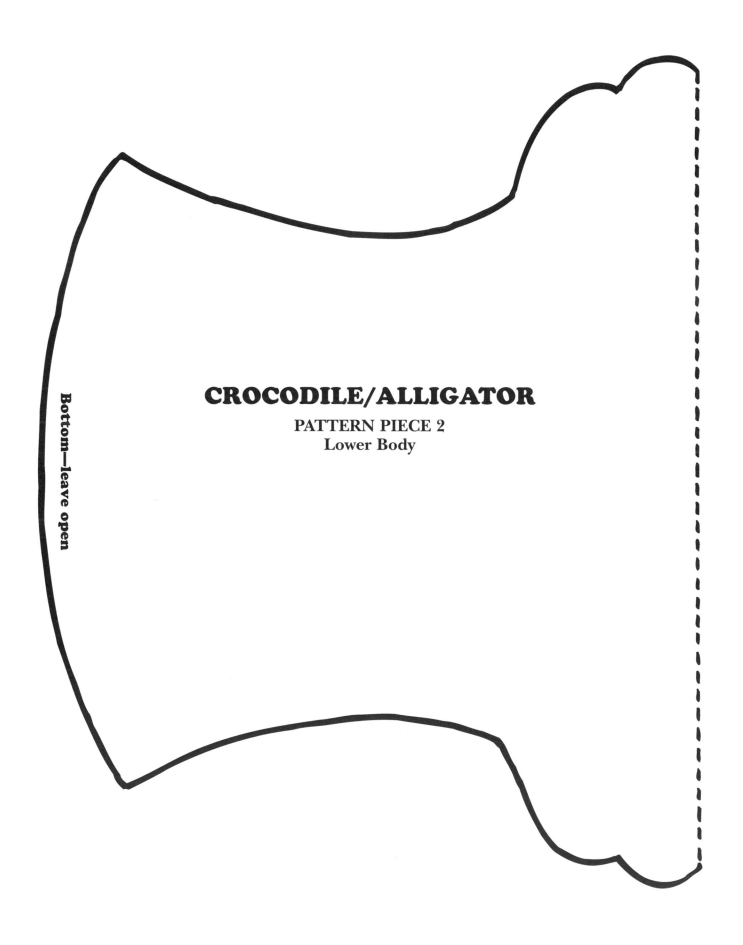

CROCODILE/ALLIGATOR

PATTERN PIECE 2
Lower Body

Bottom—leave open

CROCODILE/ALLIGATOR

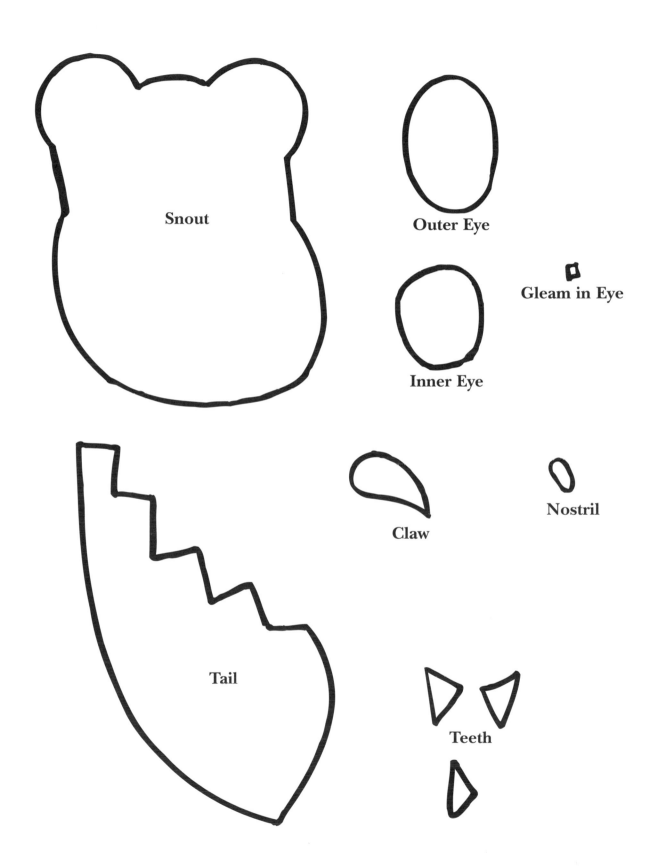

Snout

Outer Eye

Gleam in Eye

Inner Eye

Claw

Nostril

Tail

Teeth

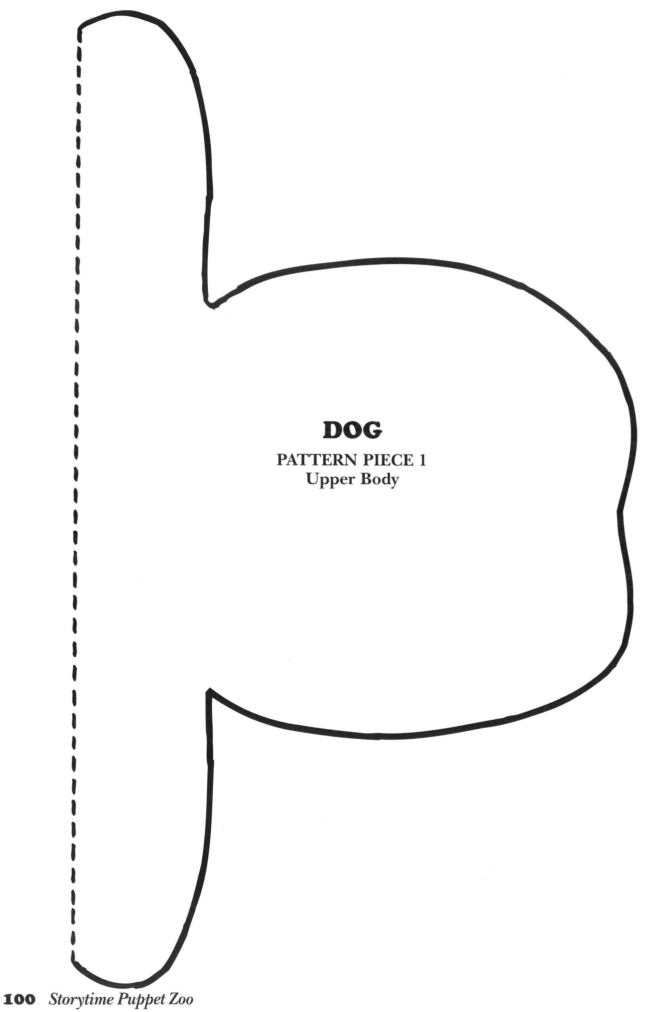

DOG

PATTERN PIECE 1
Upper Body

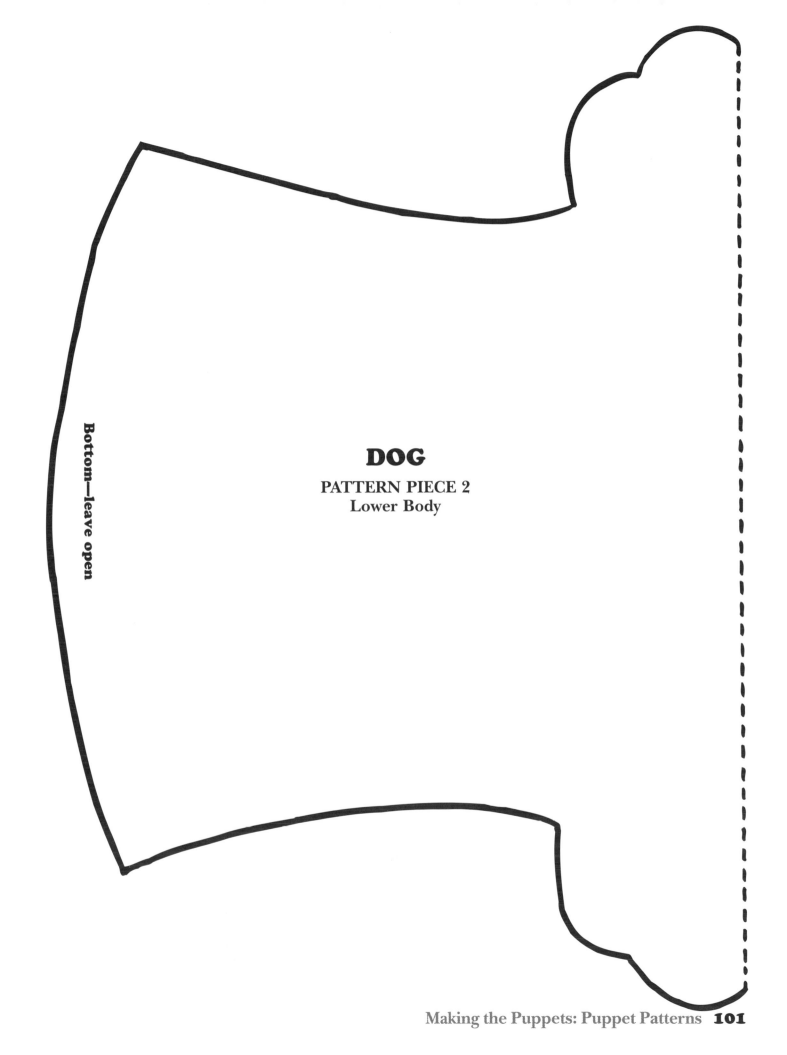

DOG

PATTERN PIECE 2
Lower Body

Bottom—leave open

DOG

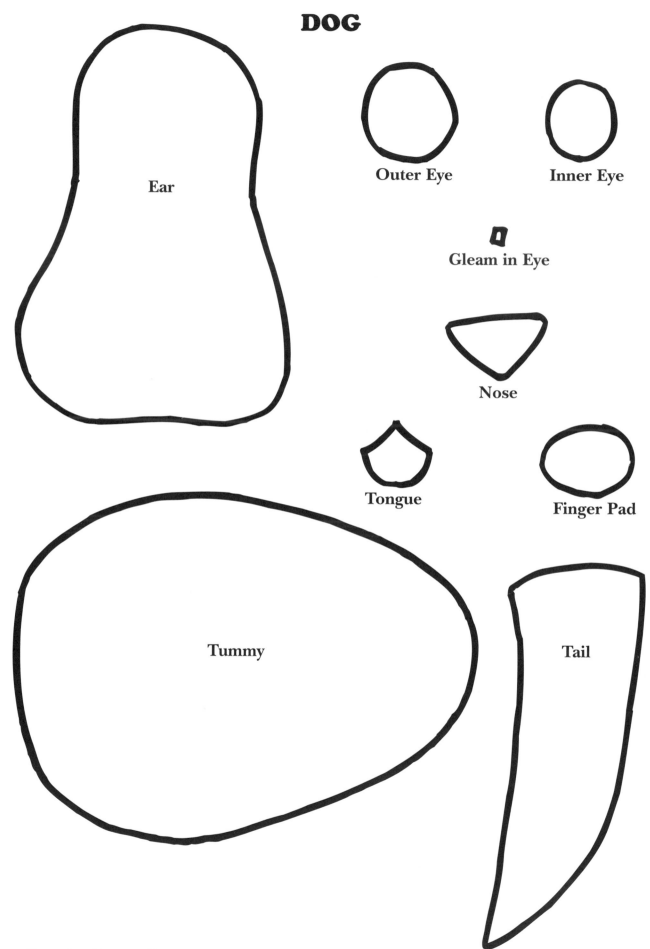

Ear

Outer Eye

Inner Eye

Gleam in Eye

Nose

Tongue

Finger Pad

Tummy

Tail

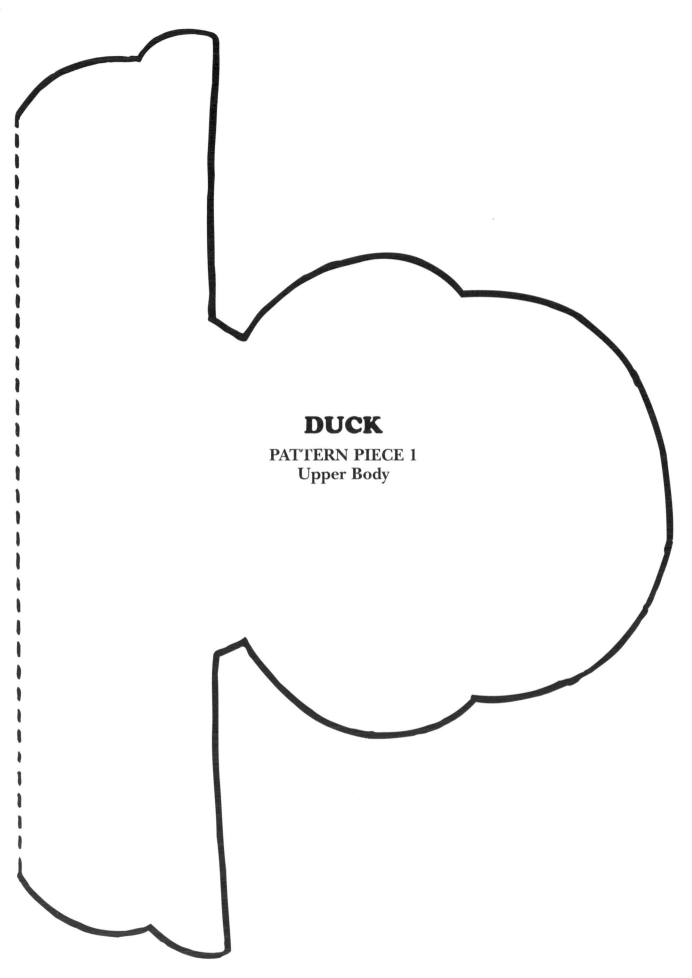

DUCK

PATTERN PIECE 1
Upper Body

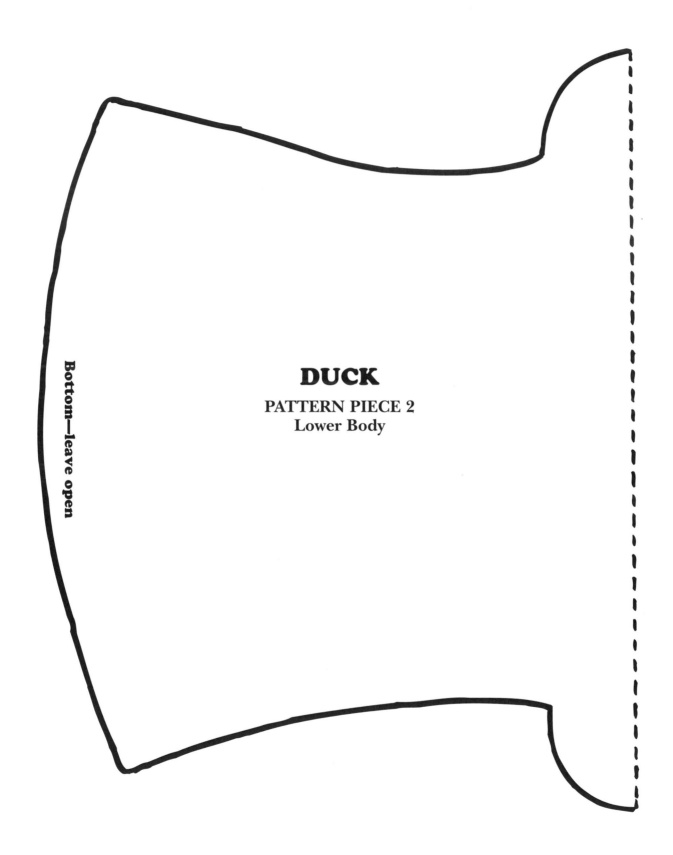

DUCK
PATTERN PIECE 2
Lower Body

Bottom—leave open

DUCK

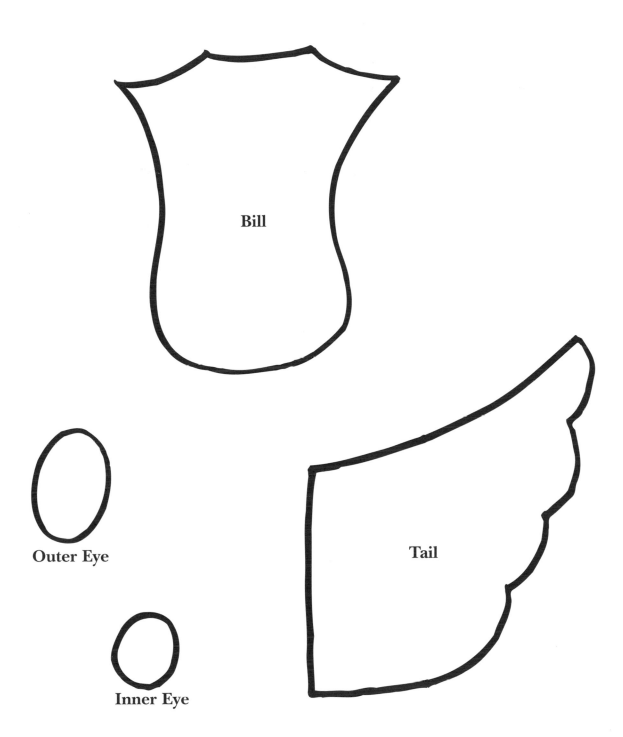

Bill

Outer Eye

Tail

Inner Eye

Gleam in Eye

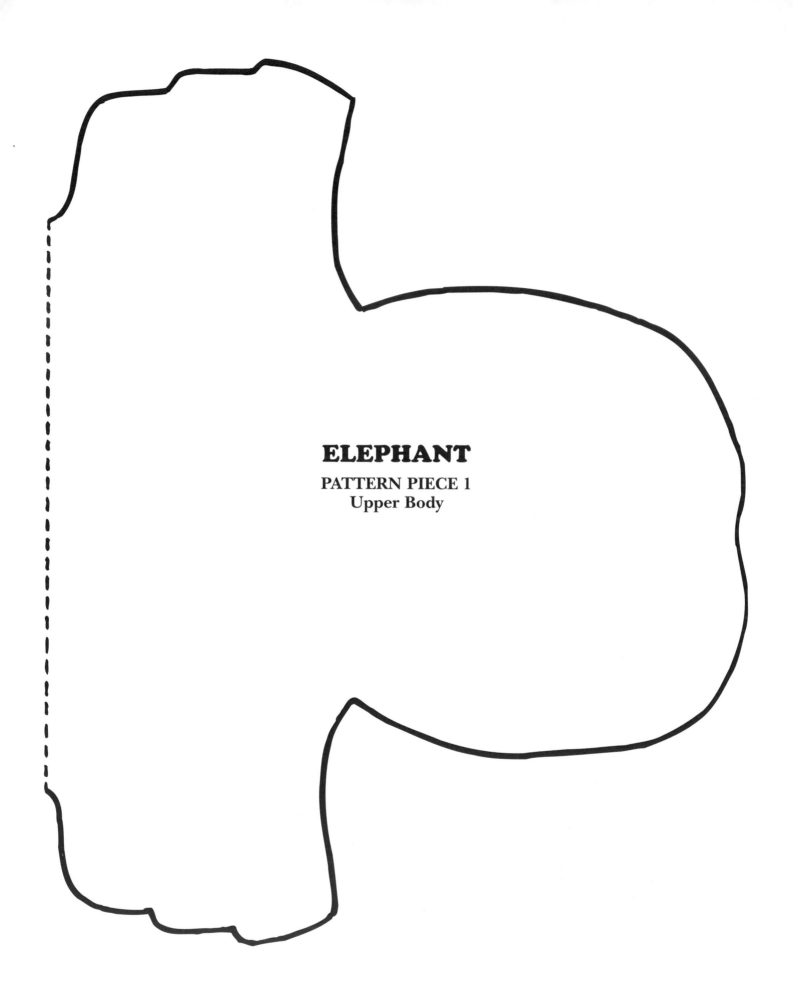

ELEPHANT

PATTERN PIECE 1
Upper Body

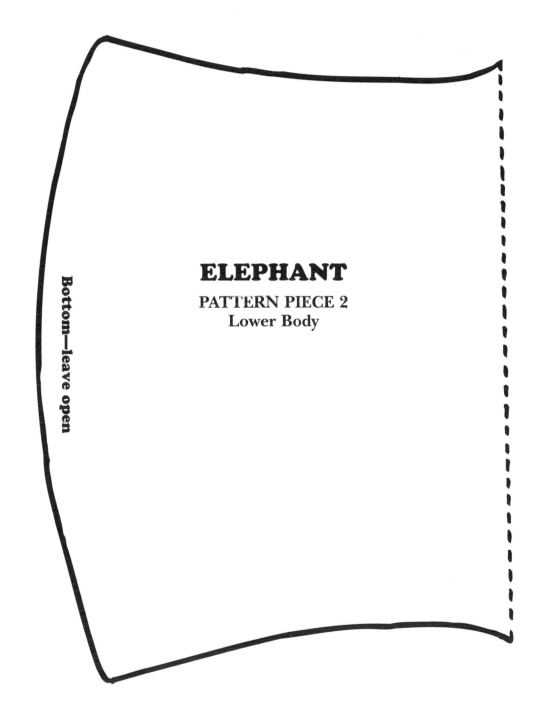

ELEPHANT

PATTERN PIECE 2
Lower Body

Bottom—leave open

ELEPHANT

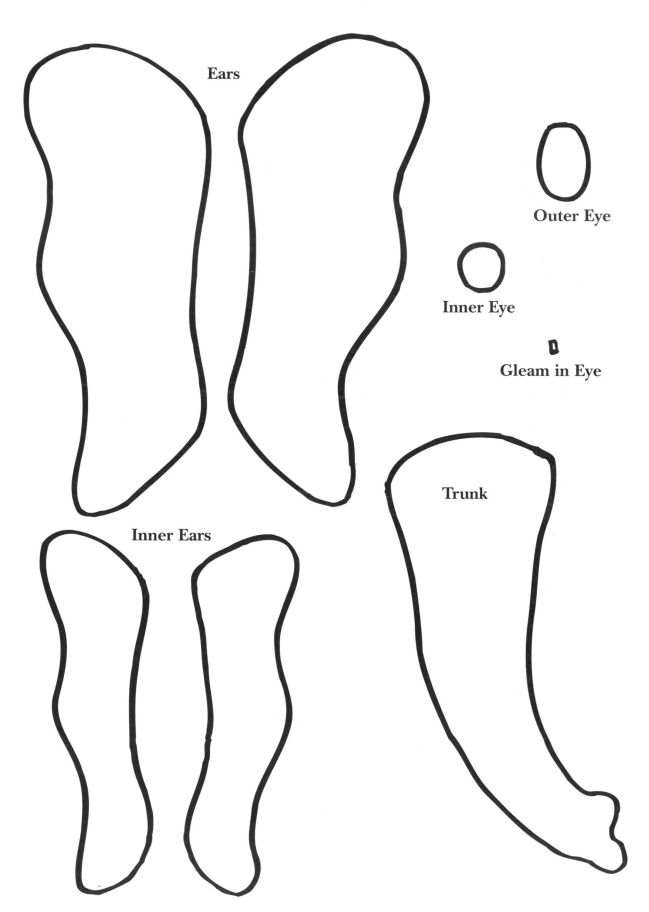

Ears

Outer Eye

Inner Eye

Gleam in Eye

Trunk

Inner Ears

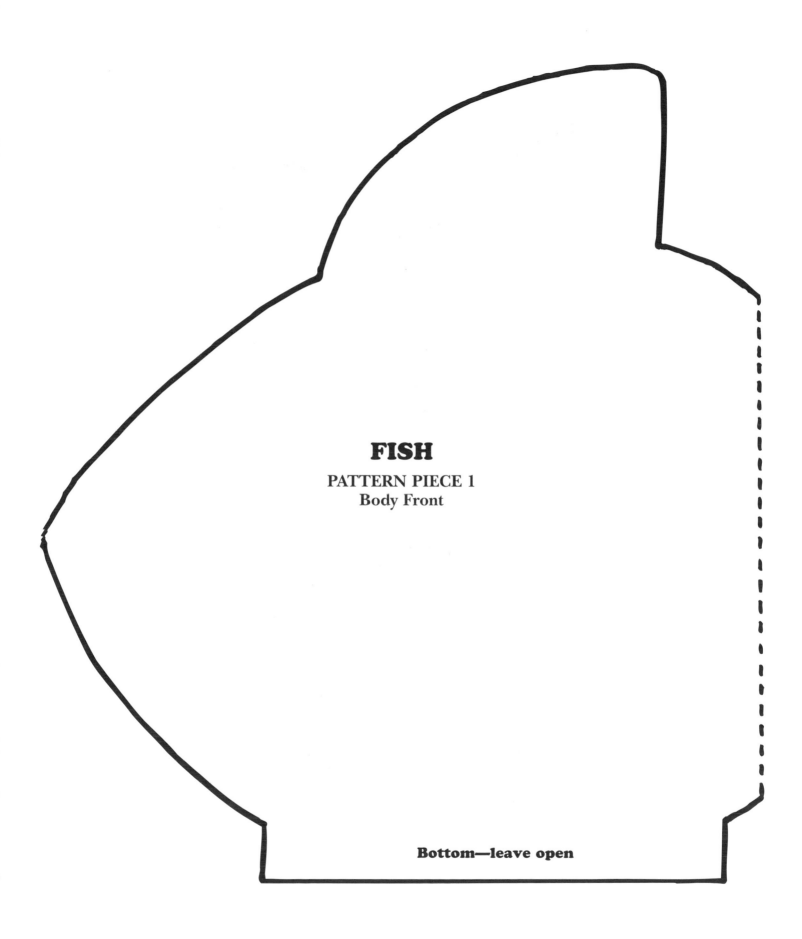

FISH

PATTERN PIECE 1
Body Front

Bottom—leave open

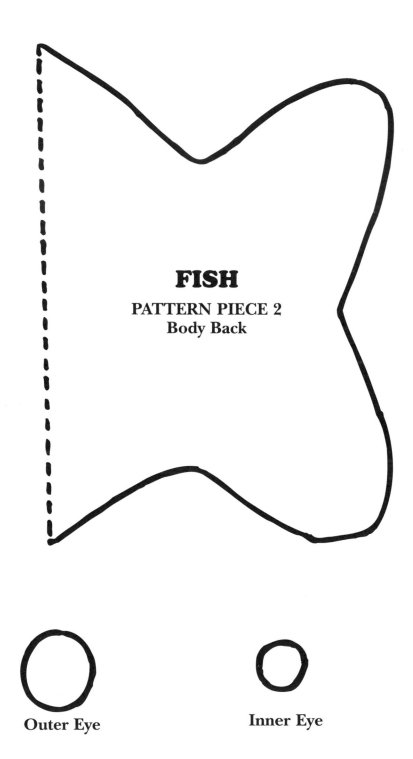

FISH

PATTERN PIECE 2
Body Back

Outer Eye

Inner Eye

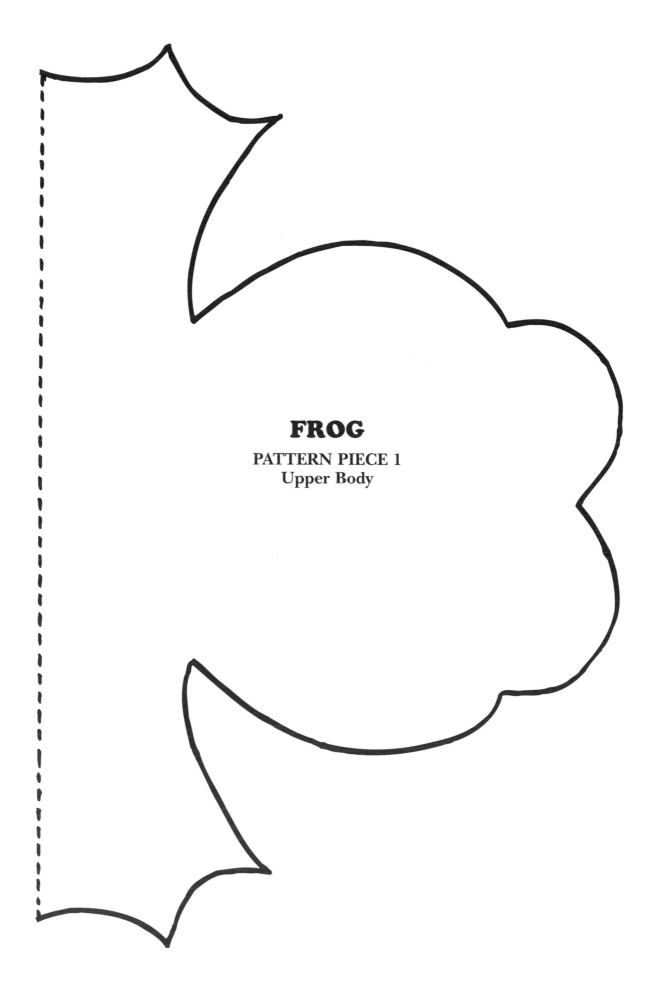

FROG

PATTERN PIECE 1
Upper Body

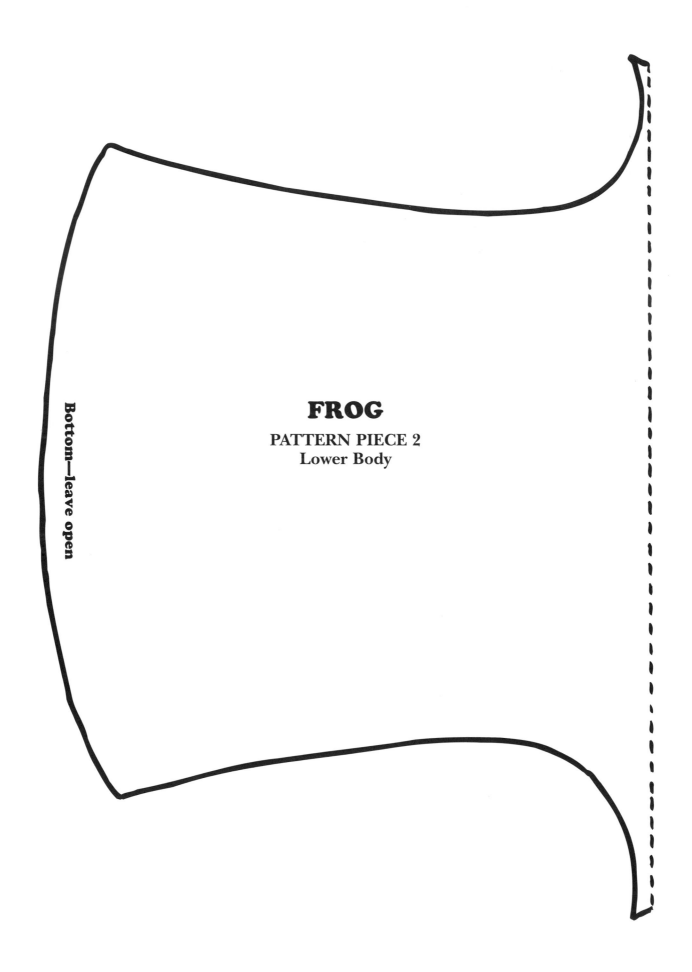

FROG
PATTERN PIECE 2
Lower Body

Bottom—leave open

FROG

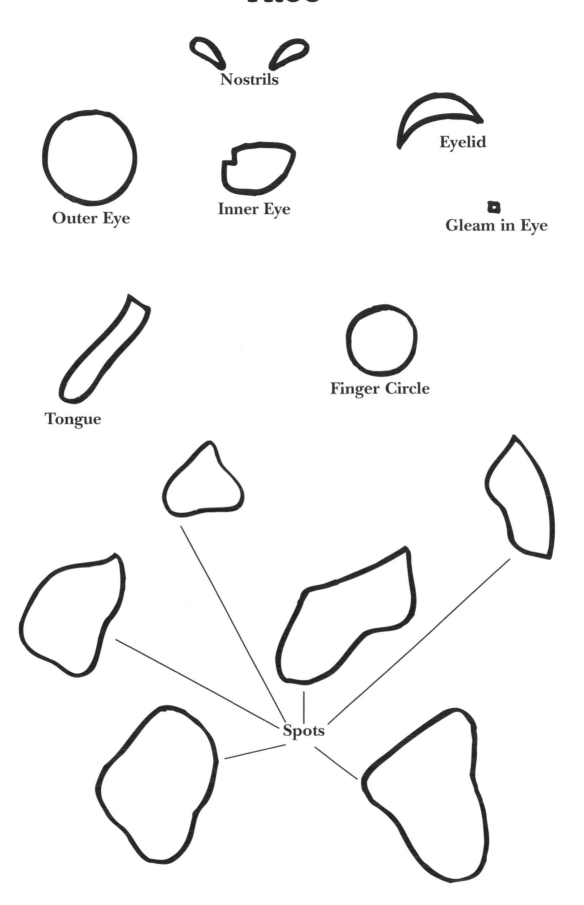

Nostrils

Eyelid

Outer Eye

Inner Eye

Gleam in Eye

Tongue

Finger Circle

Spots

HIPPOPOTAMUS

PATTERN PIECE 1
Upper Body

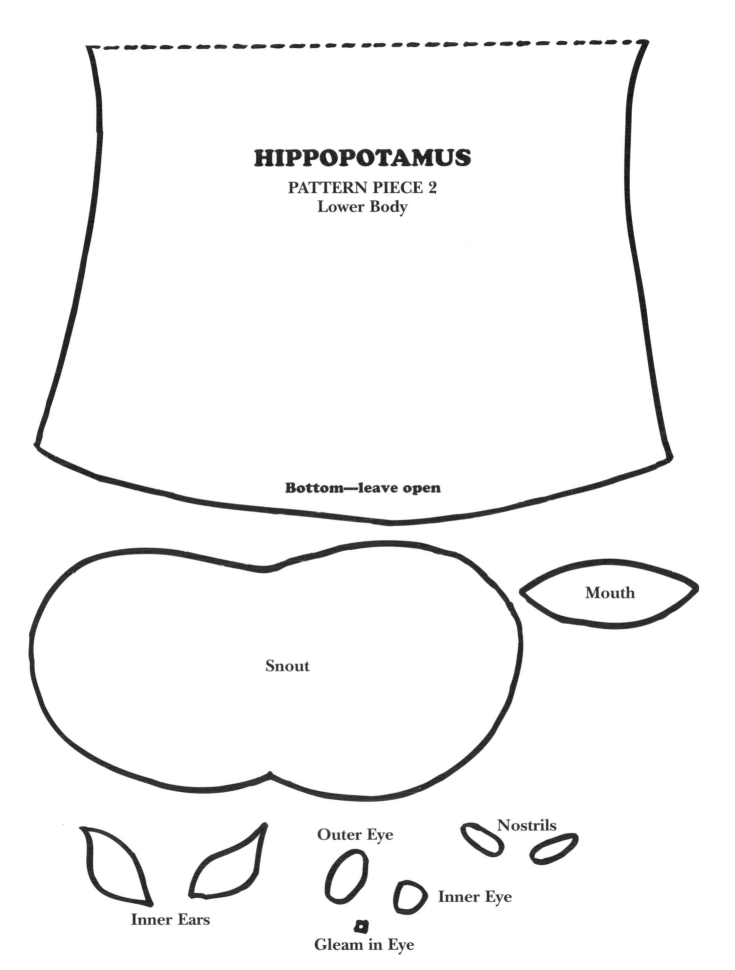

HIPPOPOTAMUS

PATTERN PIECE 2
Lower Body

Bottom—leave open

Mouth

Snout

Outer Eye

Nostrils

Inner Eye

Inner Ears

Gleam in Eye

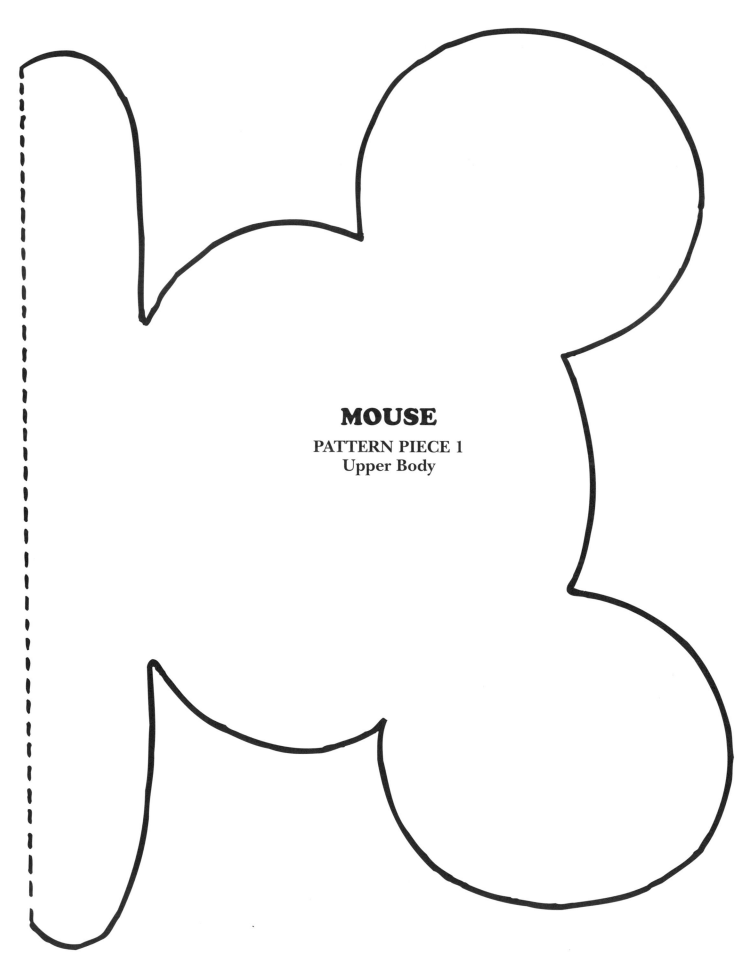

MOUSE
PATTERN PIECE 1
Upper Body

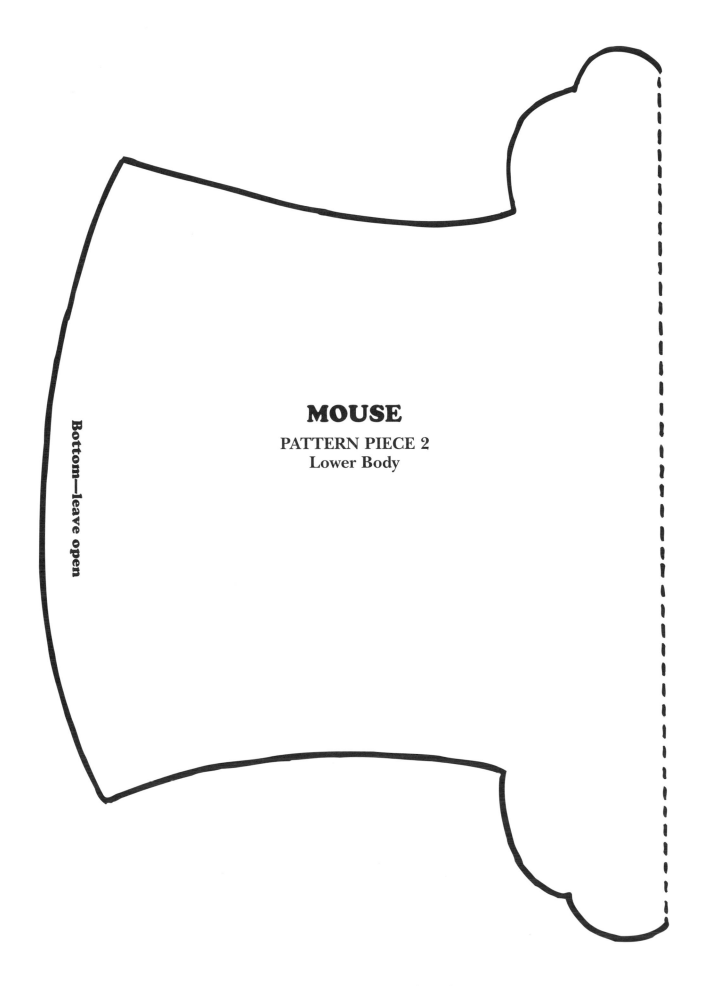

MOUSE

PATTERN PIECE 2
Lower Body

Bottom—leave open

MOUSE

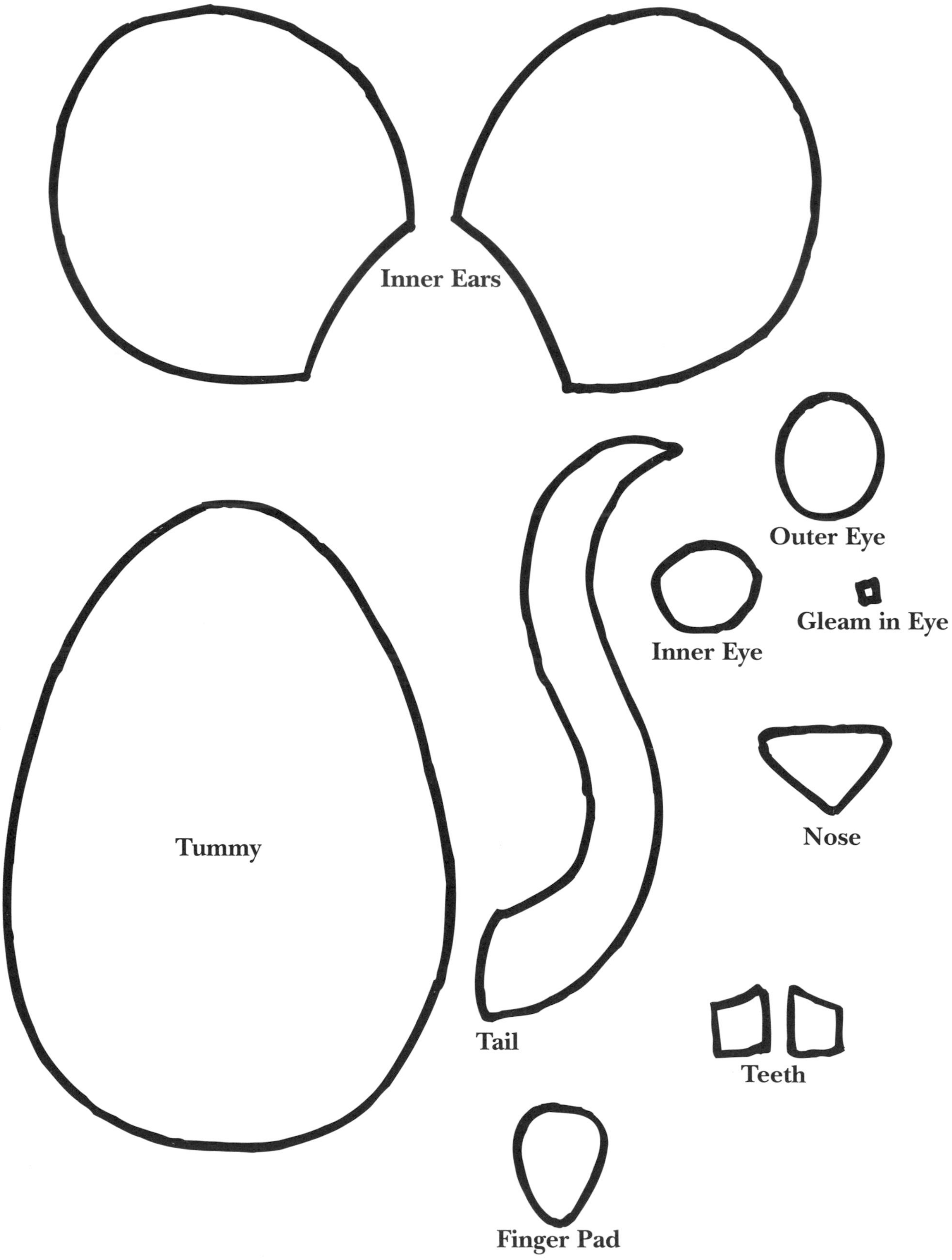

Inner Ears

Outer Eye

Gleam in Eye

Inner Eye

Tummy

Nose

Tail

Teeth

Finger Pad

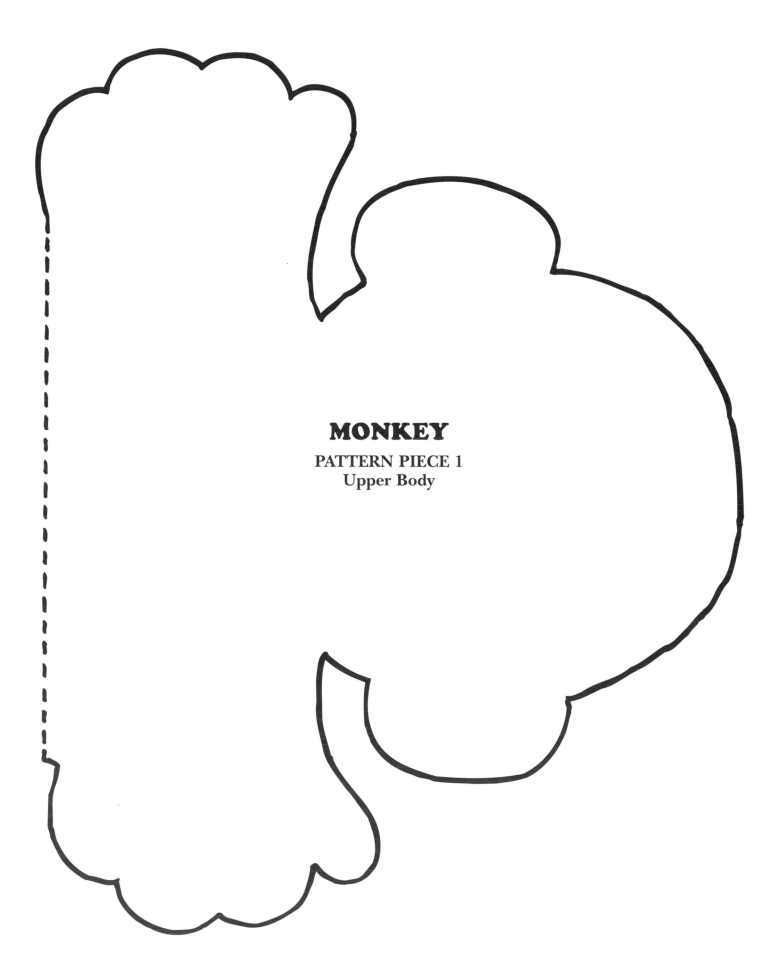

MONKEY

PATTERN PIECE 1
Upper Body

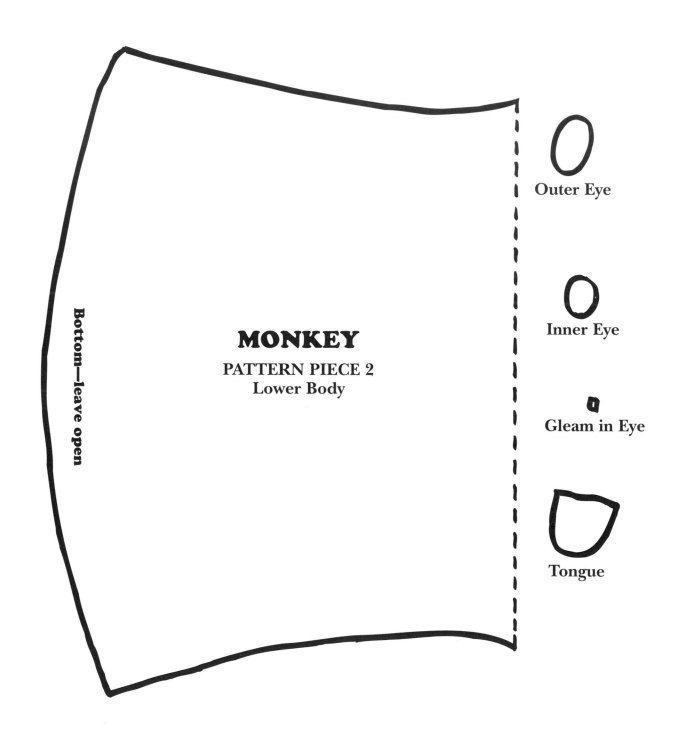

MONKEY

PATTERN PIECE 2
Lower Body

Bottom—leave open

Outer Eye

Inner Eye

Gleam in Eye

Tongue

MONKEY

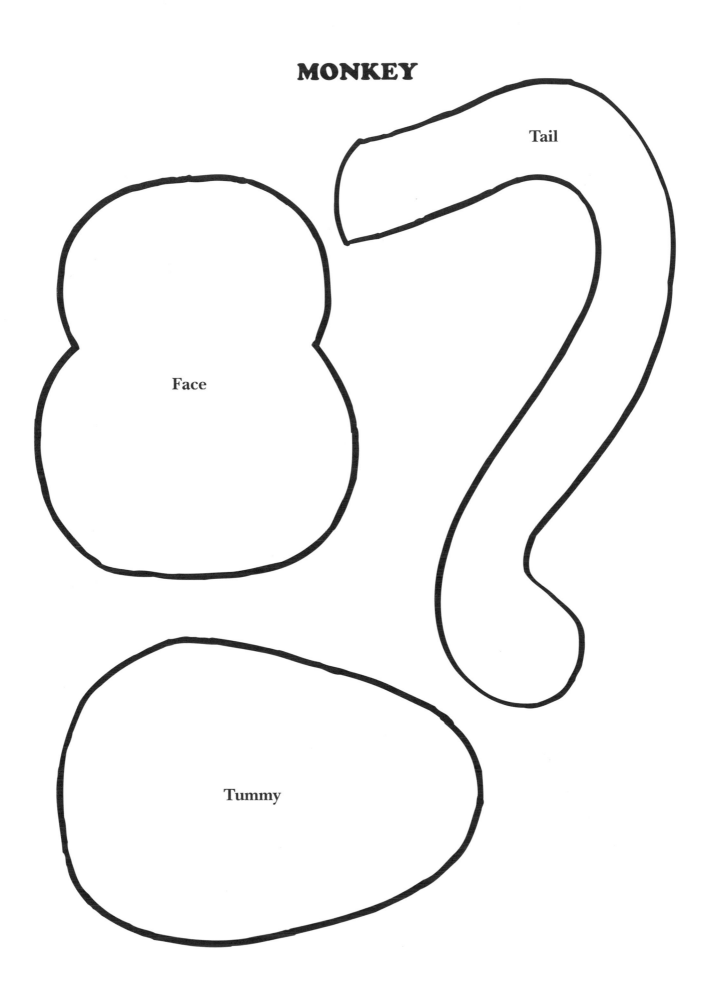

Tail

Face

Tummy

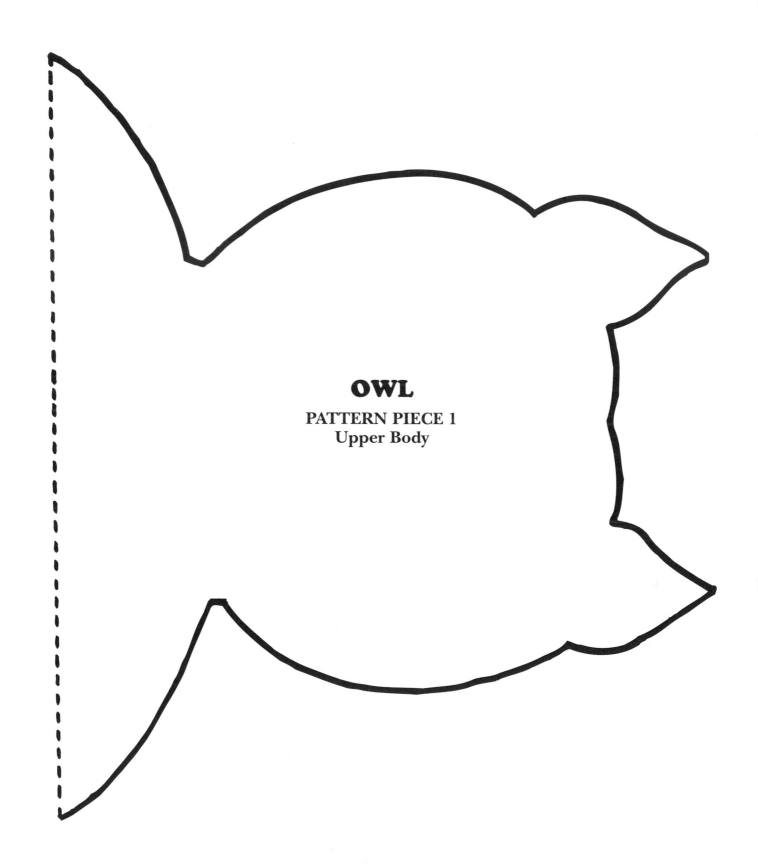

OWL

PATTERN PIECE 1
Upper Body

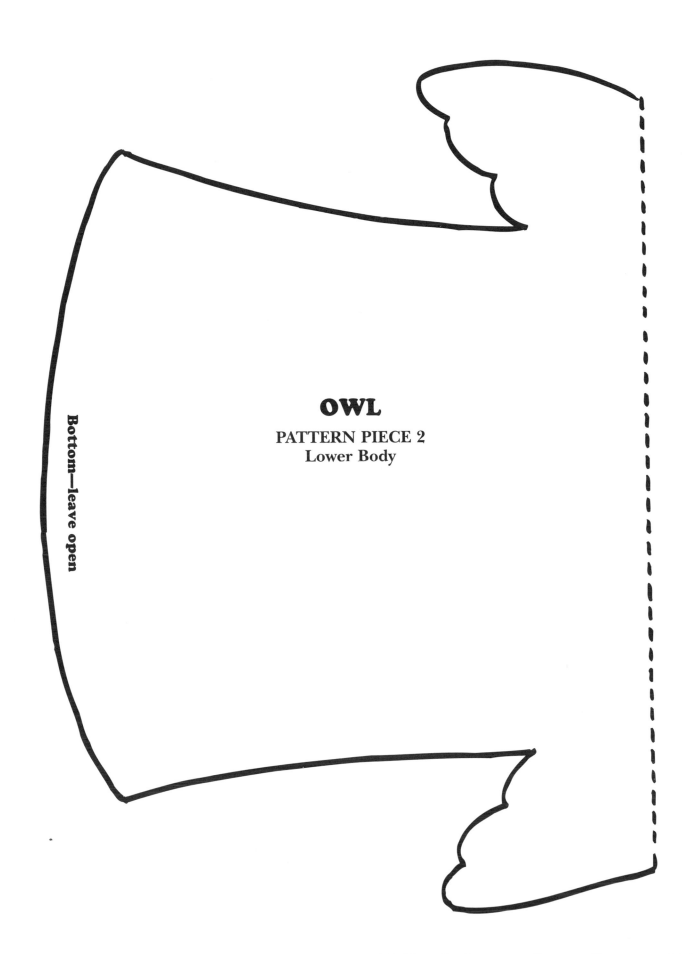

OWL

PATTERN PIECE 2
Lower Body

Bottom—leave open

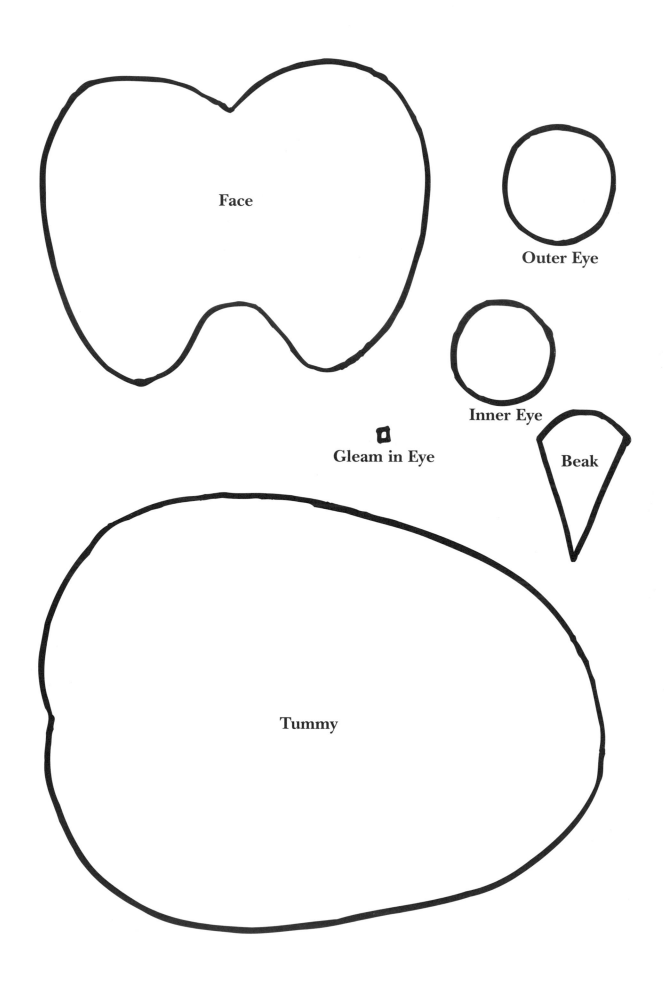

Face

Outer Eye

Inner Eye

Gleam in Eye

Beak

Tummy

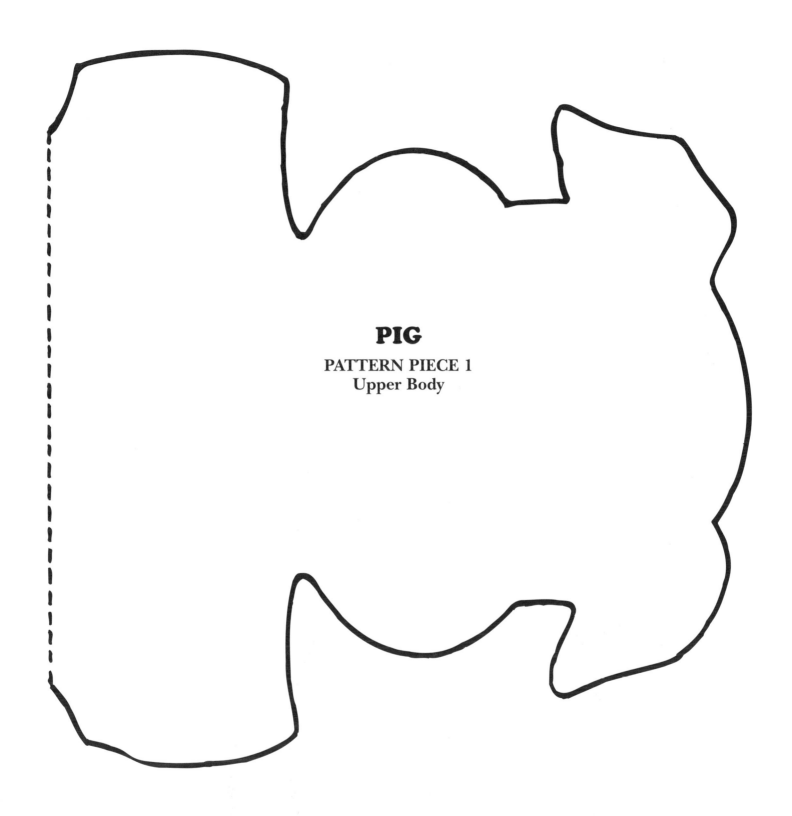

PIG
PATTERN PIECE 1
Upper Body

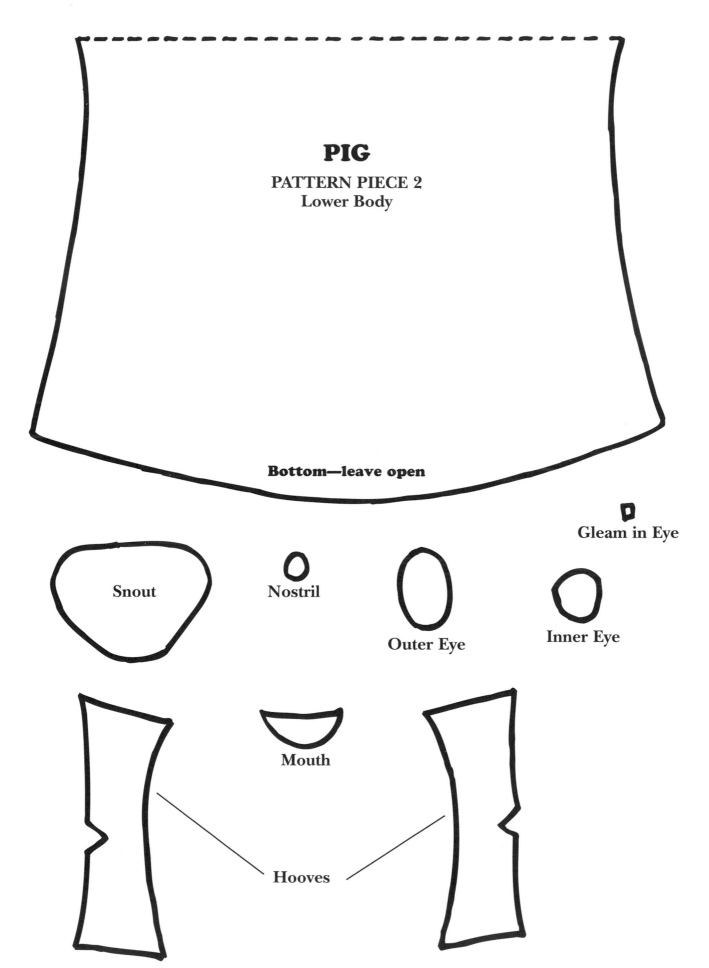

PIG

PATTERN PIECE 2
Lower Body

Bottom—leave open

Gleam in Eye

Snout

Nostril

Outer Eye

Inner Eye

Mouth

Hooves

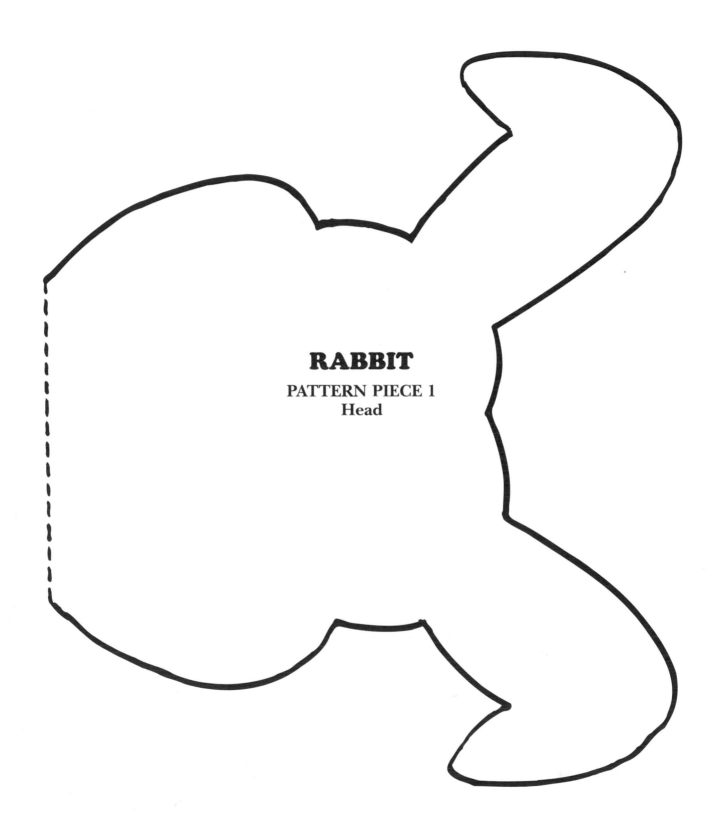

RABBIT

PATTERN PIECE 1
Head

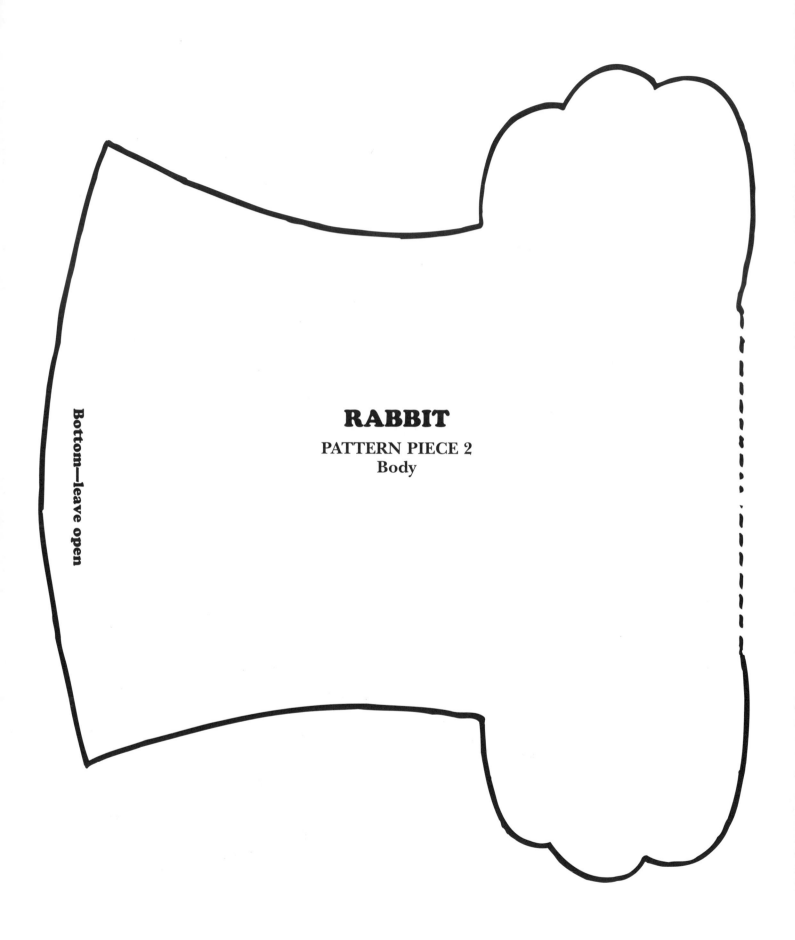

RABBIT

PATTERN PIECE 2
Body

Bottom—leave open

RABBIT

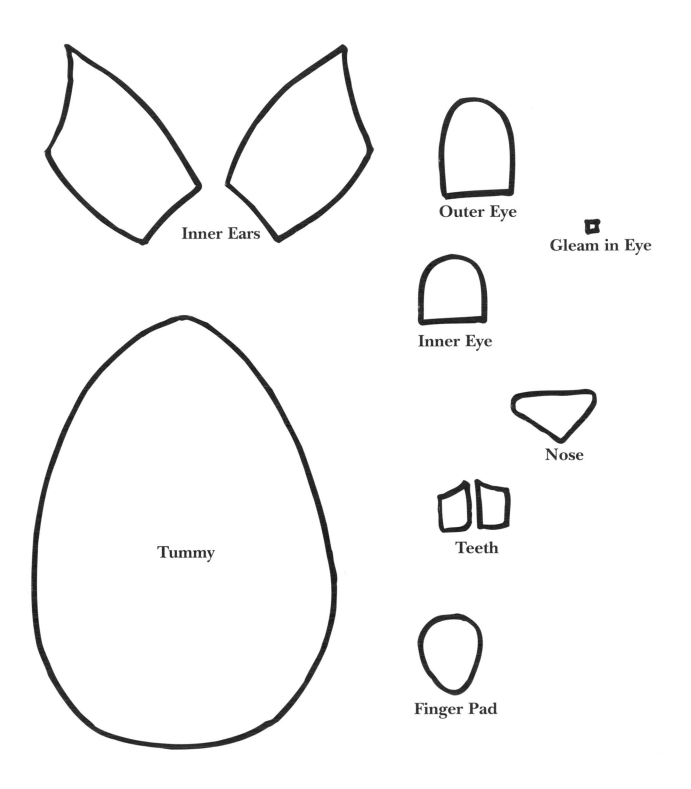

Inner Ears

Outer Eye

Gleam in Eye

Inner Eye

Nose

Tummy

Teeth

Finger Pad

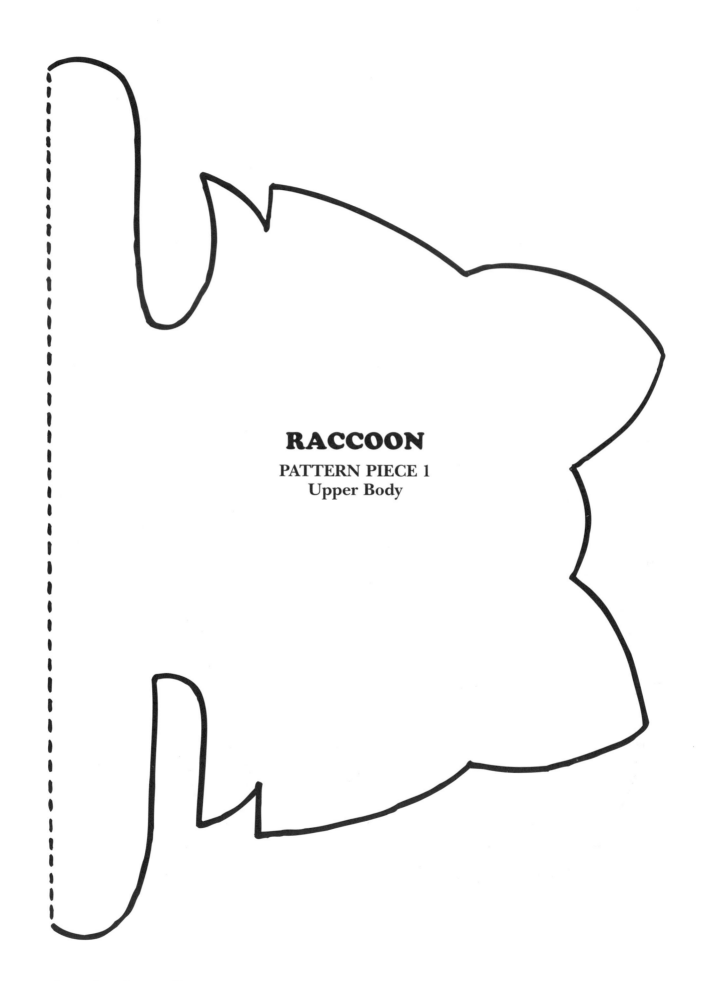

RACCOON

PATTERN PIECE 1
Upper Body

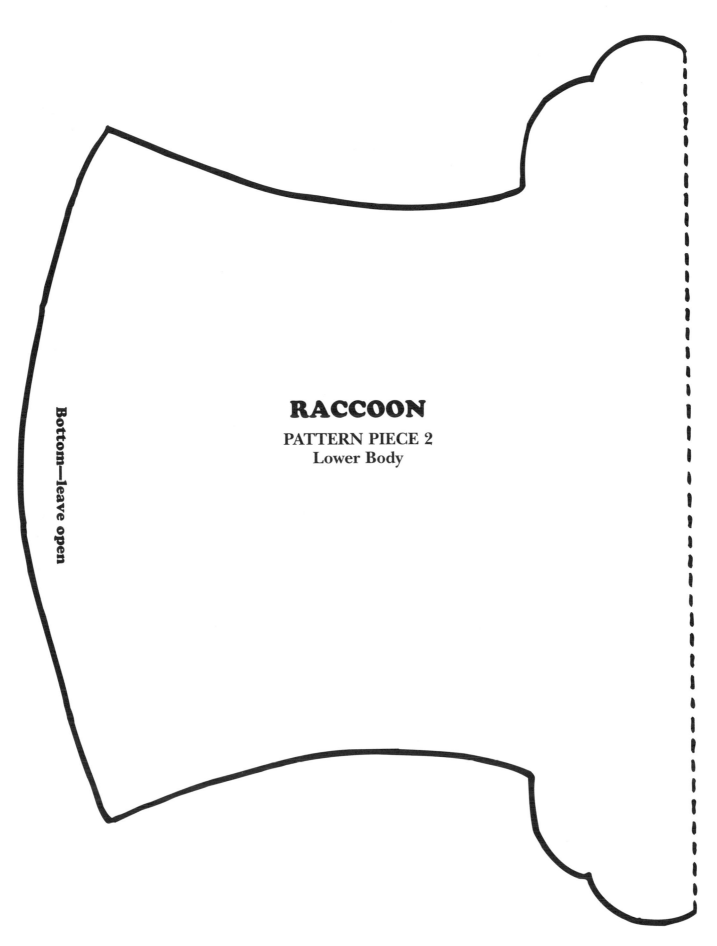

RACCOON

PATTERN PIECE 2
Lower Body

Bottom—leave open

RACCOON

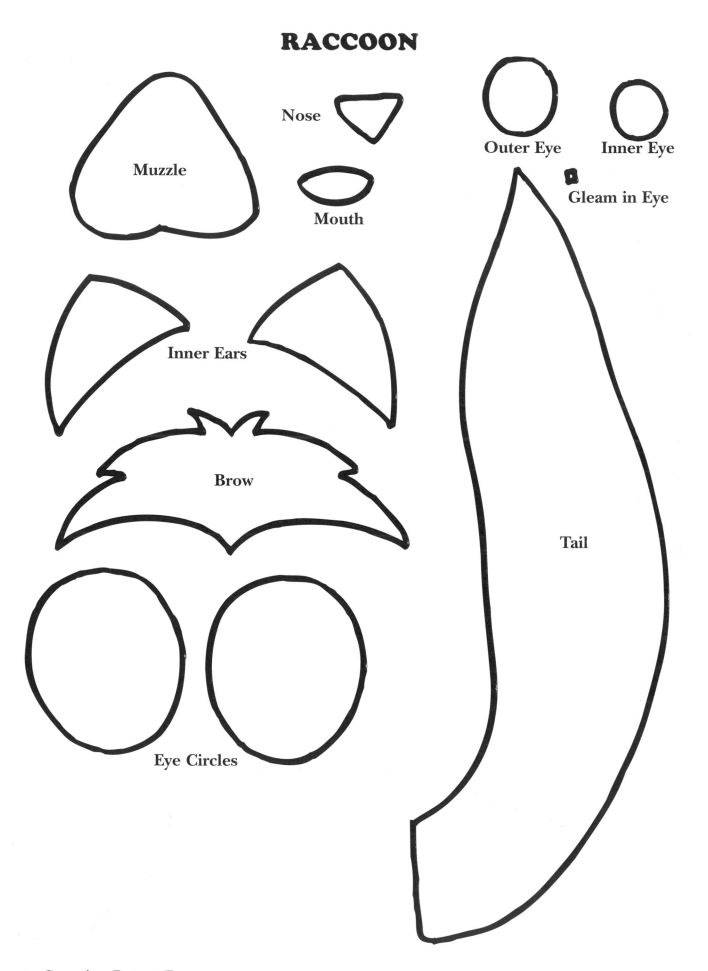

Nose

Muzzle

Mouth

Outer Eye

Inner Eye

Gleam in Eye

Inner Ears

Brow

Tail

Eye Circles

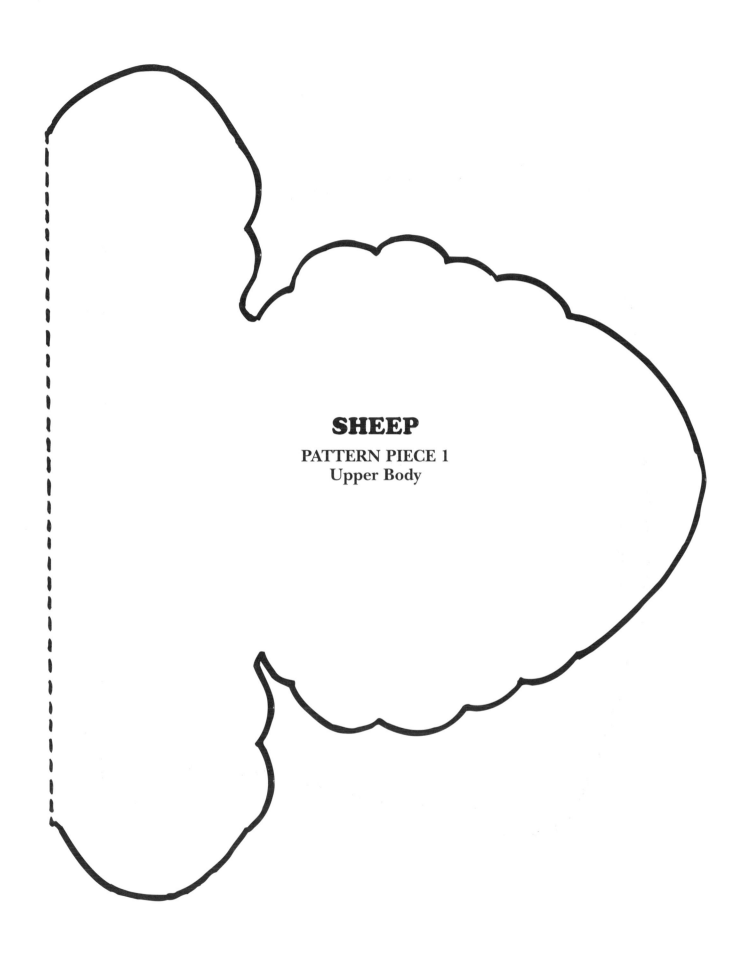

SHEEP

PATTERN PIECE 1
Upper Body

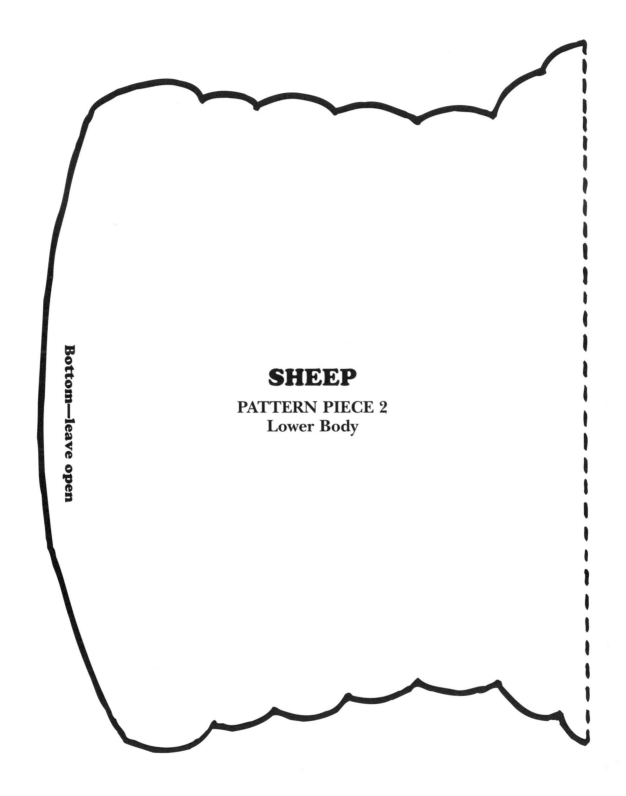

SHEEP

PATTERN PIECE 2
Lower Body

Bottom—leave open

SHEEP

Head Top

Ear

Ear

Lip

Muzzle

Inner Ears

Eyelid

Hooves

SKUNK

PATTERN PIECE 1
Upper Body

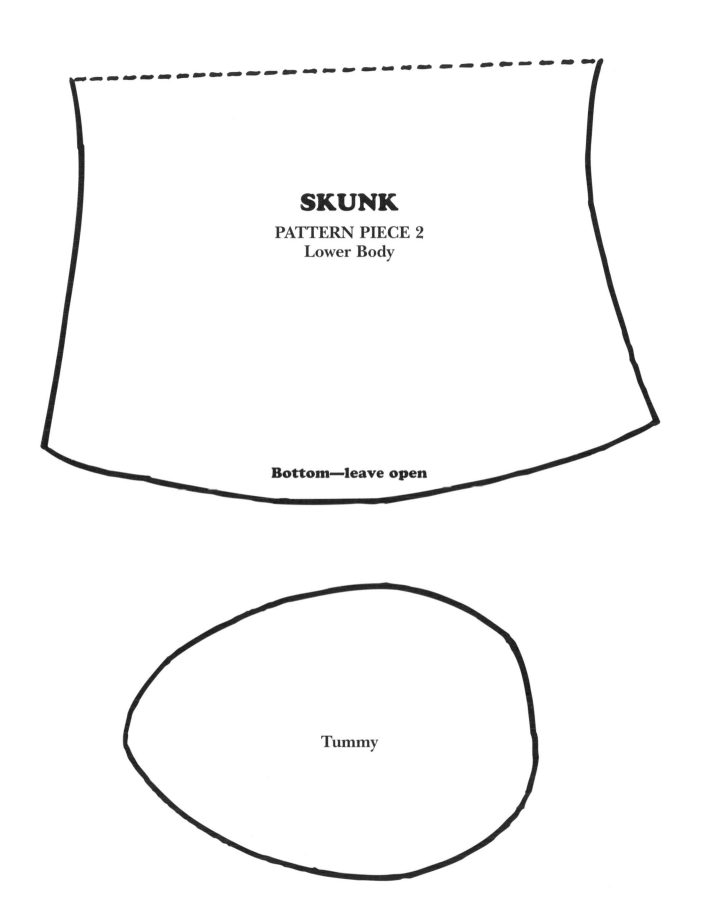

SKUNK

PATTERN PIECE 2
Lower Body

Bottom—leave open

Tummy

SKUNK

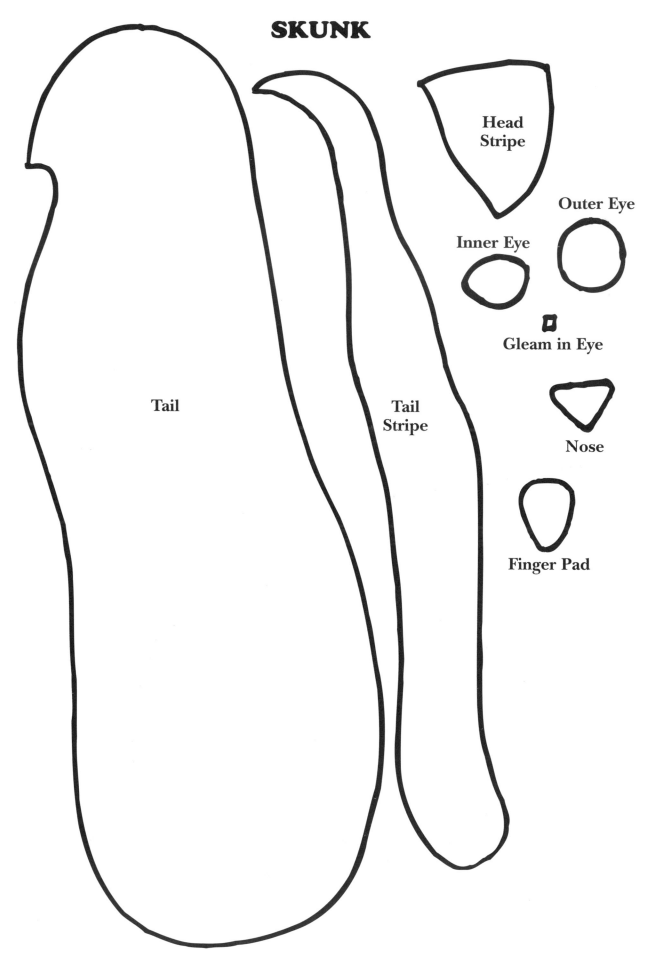

Tail

Tail
Stripe

Head
Stripe

Outer Eye

Inner Eye

Gleam in Eye

Nose

Finger Pad

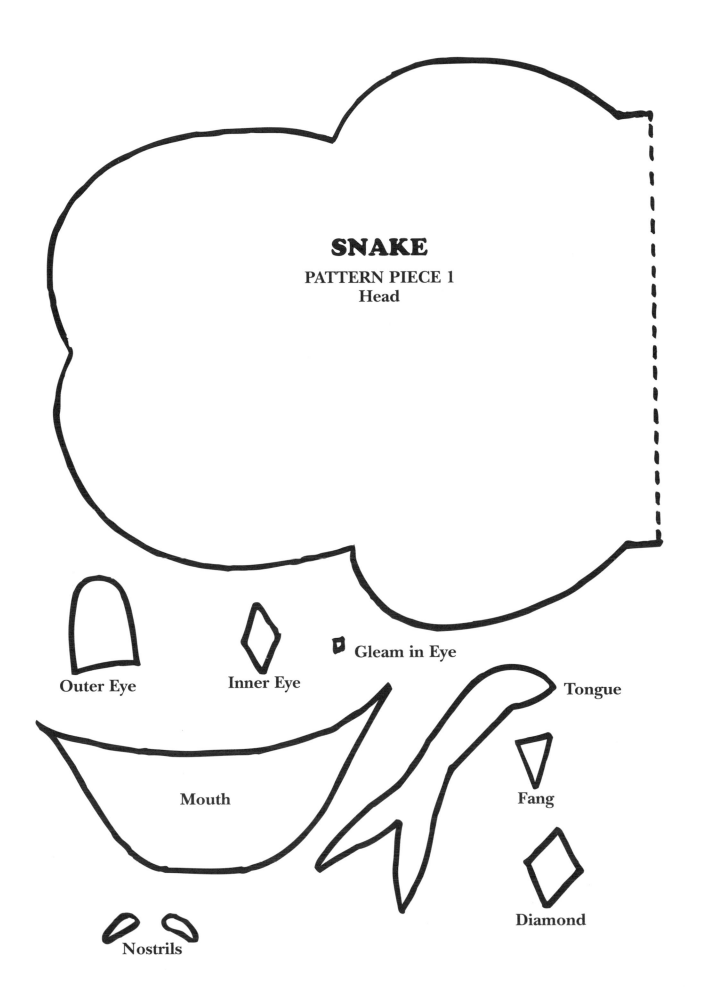

SNAKE

PATTERN PIECE 1
Head

Gleam in Eye

Outer Eye

Inner Eye

Tongue

Mouth

Fang

Diamond

Nostrils

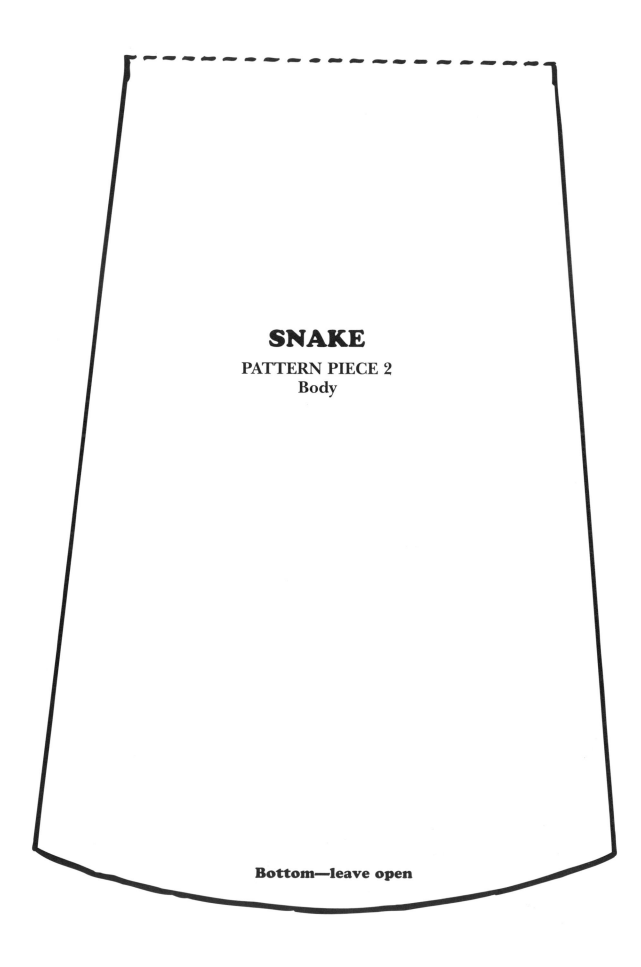

SNAKE

PATTERN PIECE 2
Body

Bottom—leave open

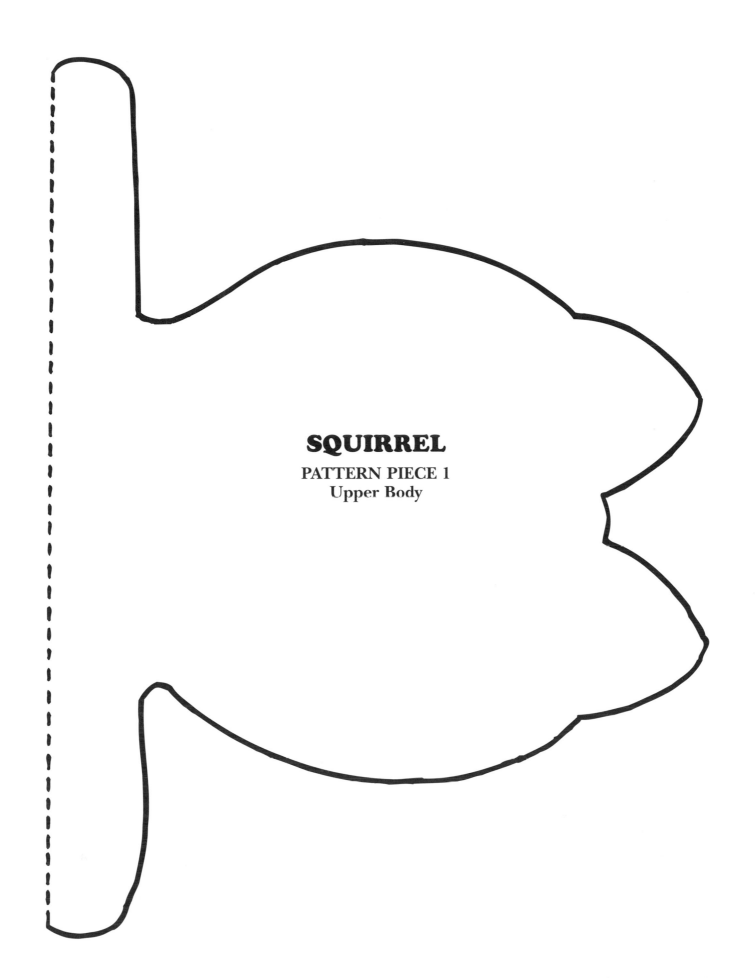

SQUIRREL

PATTERN PIECE 1
Upper Body

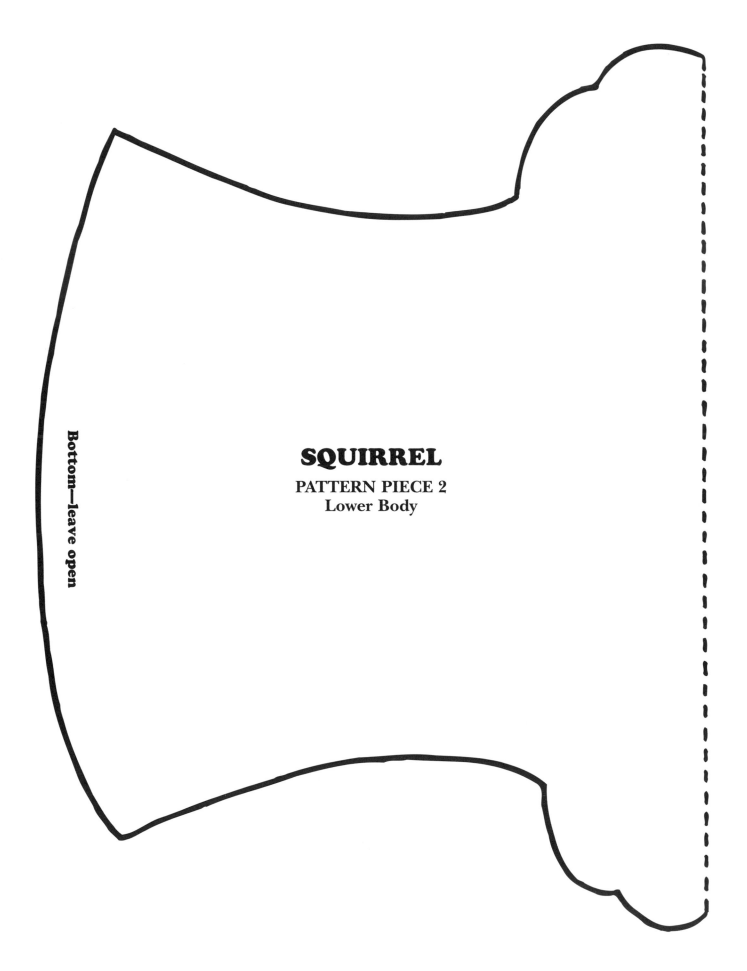

SQUIRREL

PATTERN PIECE 2
Lower Body

Bottom—leave open

SQUIRREL

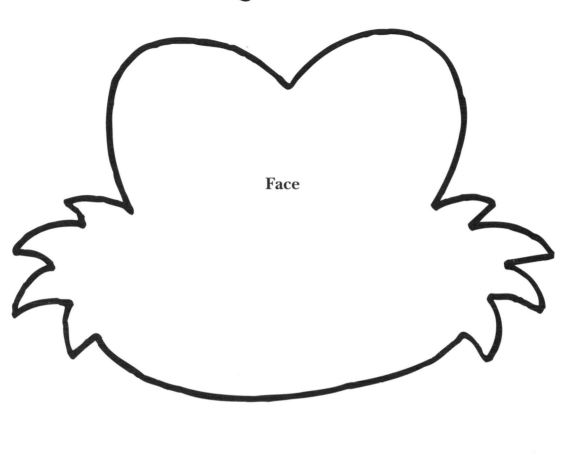

Face

Outer Eye

Inner Eye

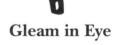

Gleam in Eye

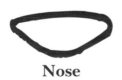

Nose

Teeth

SQUIRREL

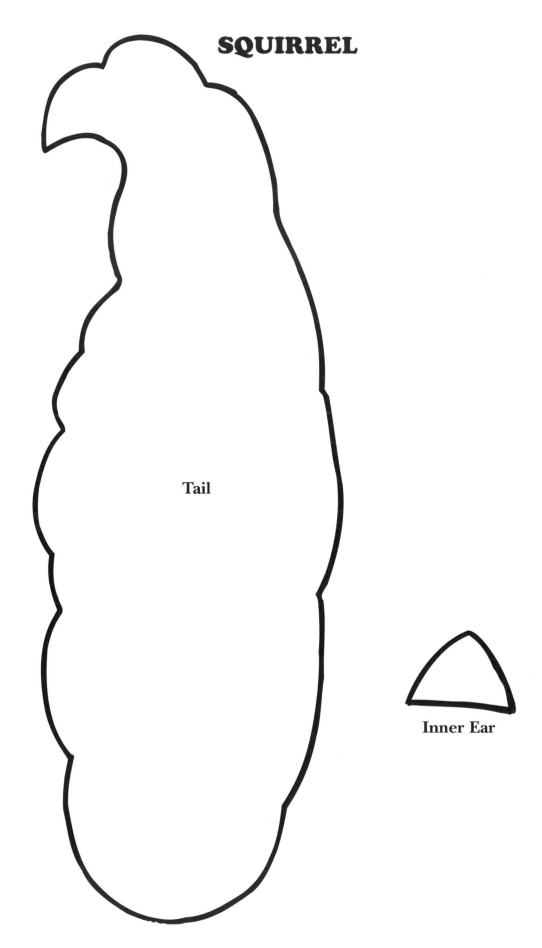

Tail

Inner Ear

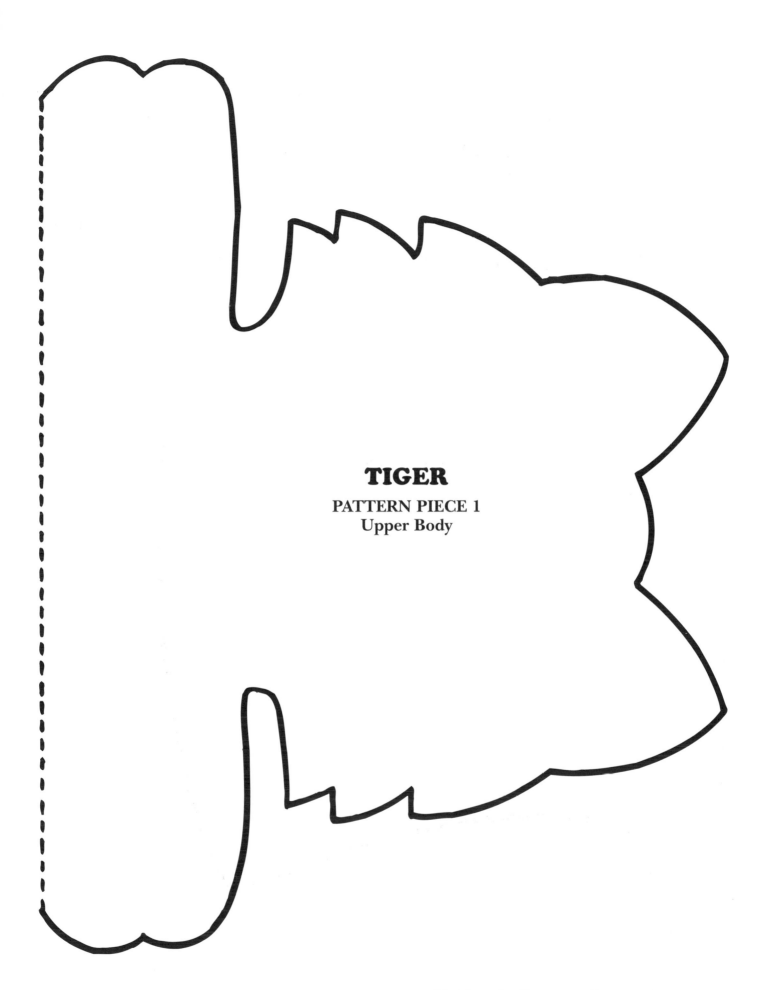

TIGER

PATTERN PIECE 1
Upper Body

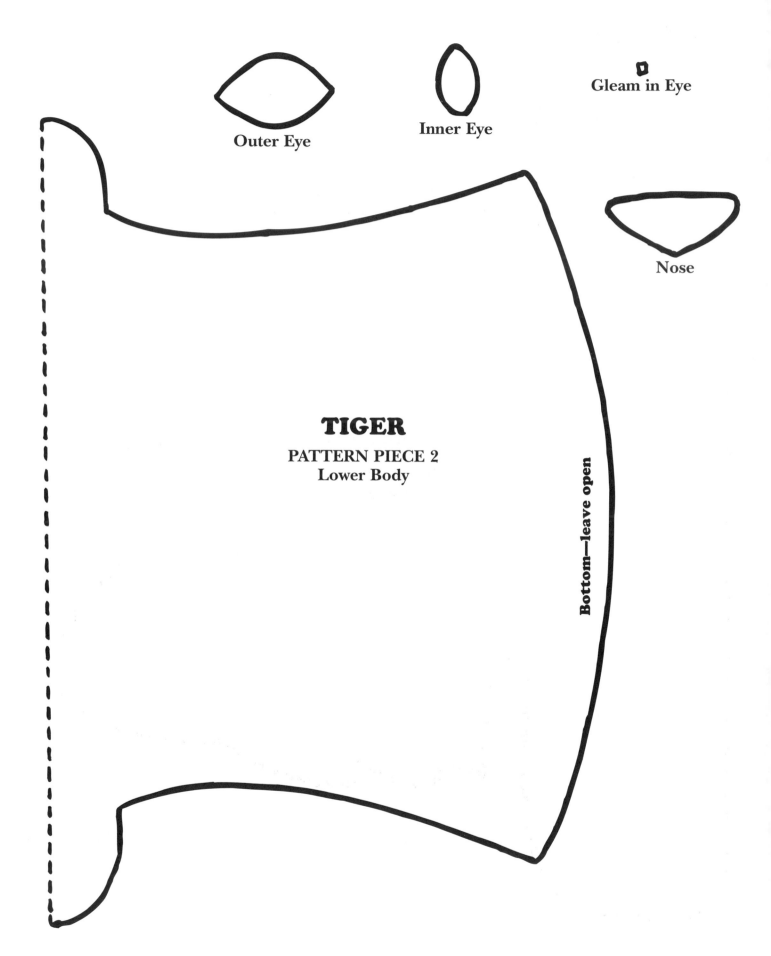

Outer Eye

Inner Eye

Gleam in Eye

Nose

TIGER

PATTERN PIECE 2
Lower Body

Bottom—leave open

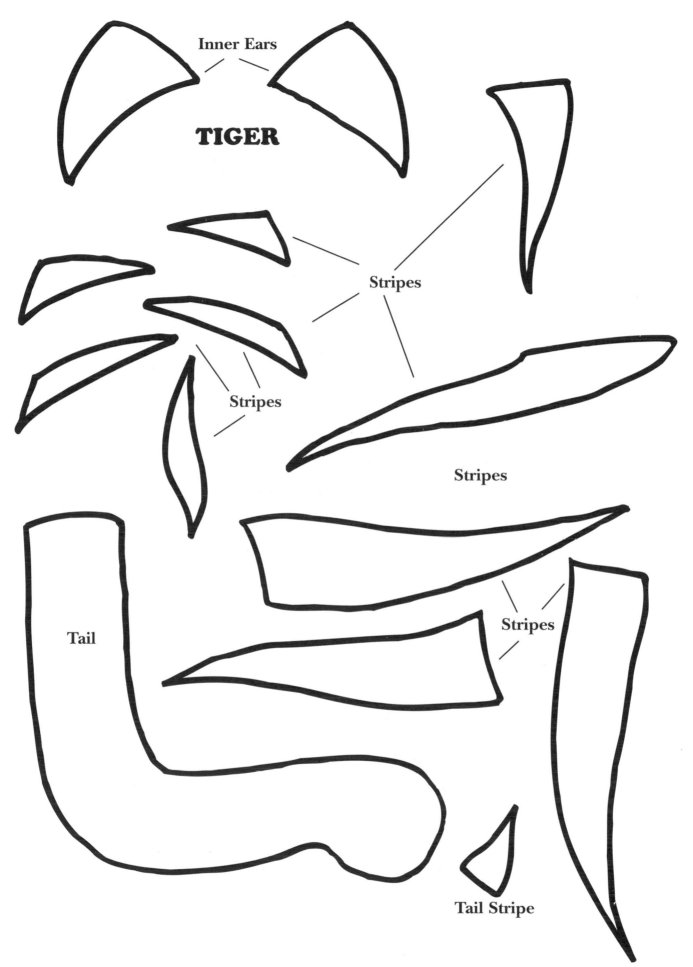

Inner Ears

TIGER

Stripes

Stripes

Stripes

Stripes

Tail

Tail Stripe

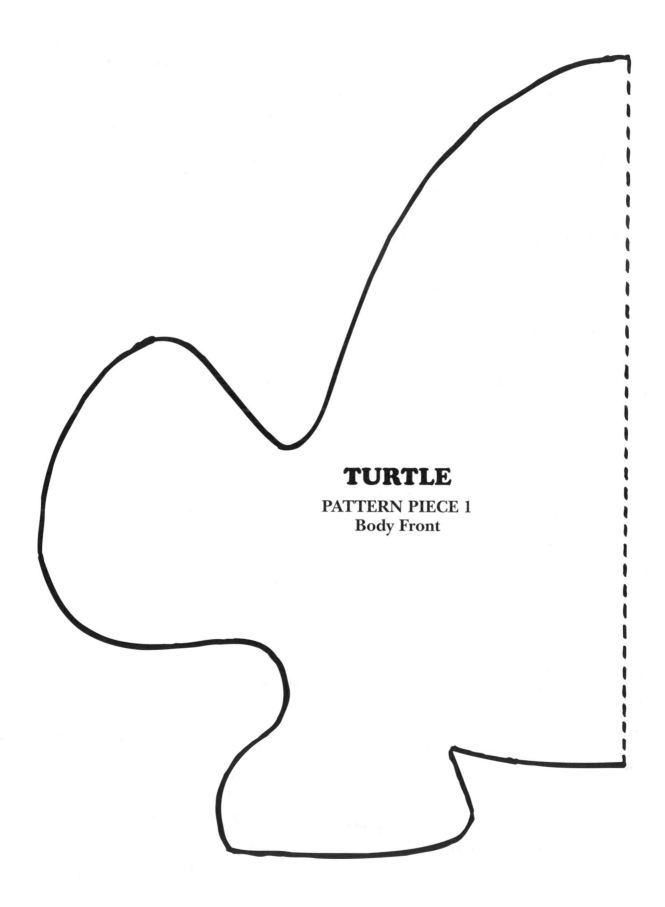

TURTLE

PATTERN PIECE 1
Body Front

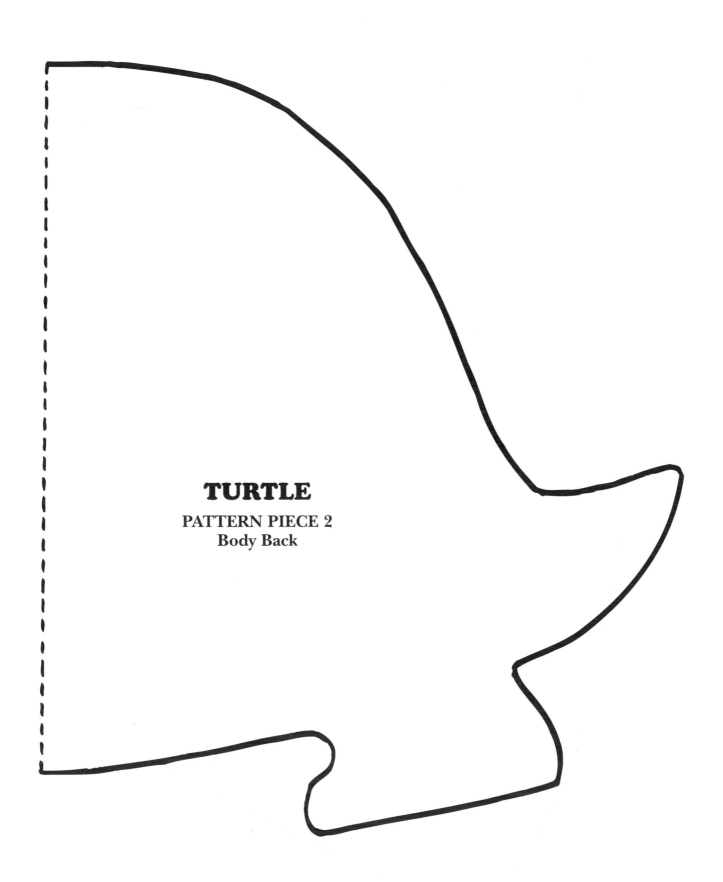

TURTLE

PATTERN PIECE 2
Body Back

TURTLE

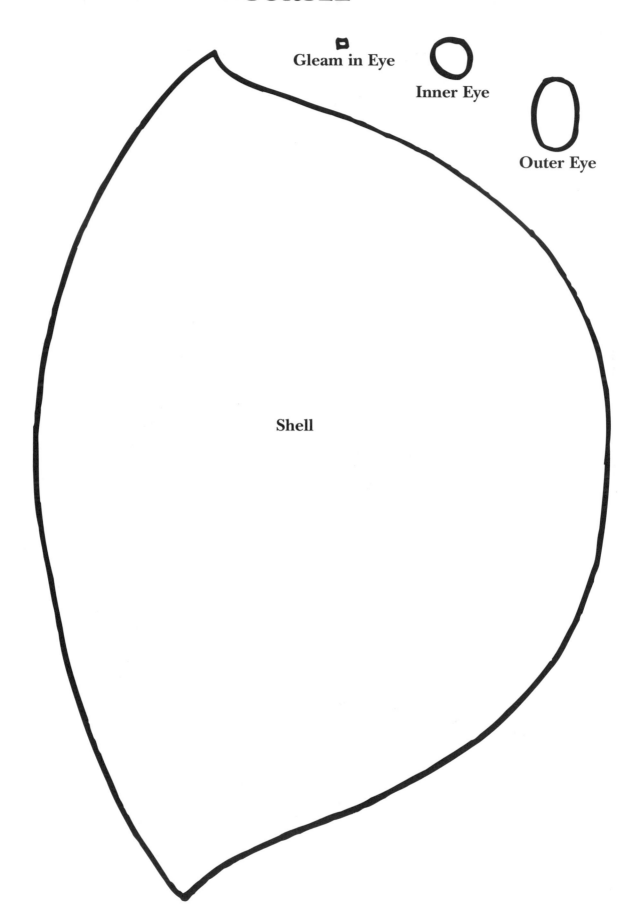

Gleam in Eye

Inner Eye

Outer Eye

Shell

Additional Resources on Puppetry

Anderson, Dee. *Amazingly Easy Puppet Plays: 42 New Scripts for One-Person Puppetry.* American Library Association, 1996. Puppet skits for single puppeteers.

Astell-Burt, Caroline. *I Am the Story.* Souvenir Press, 2002. Uses puppetry for education and therapy.

Bailey, Elinor Peace. *Storytelling with Dolls.* KP Books, 2003. A unique way to present stories.

Bauer, Caroline Feller. *Leading Kids to Books through Puppets.* American Library Association, 1997. A focus on reading and storytelling through puppets.

Buetter, Barbara. *Simple Puppets from Everyday Materials.* Sterling Publishing, 1996. Directions for making puppets from easily obtainable materials.

Doney, Meryl. *Puppets.* Gareth Stevens, 2003. Puppetry as seen through other cultures and countries.

Engler, Larry. *Making Puppets Come Alive.* Dover Publications, 1996. A very good resource on puppetry, including voice, staging, lighting and more.

Haines, Ken and Gill Harvey. *The Usborne Book of Puppets.* Usborne Books, 1998. Instructions on creating puppets from everyday objects.

Kennedy, John E. *Puppet Mania!* F & W Publications, 2003. Thirteen original projects for puppets from household materials.

Latshaw, George. *The Complete Book of Puppetry.* Dover Publications, 2000. Instructional book on puppetry.

Lohnes, Marilyn. *Fractured Fairy Tales: Puppet Plays and Patterns.* UpstartBooks, 2002. Ten puppet scripts as well as both simple and professional puppet patterns.

Minkel, Walter. *How To Do "The Three Bears" with Two Hands: Performing with Puppets.* American Library Association, 2000. Simple puppet plays for one puppeteer.

Shepherd, Nellie. *My Puppet Art Class.* DK Publishing, 2003. Simple puppet making for children.

Wolf, Gita. *Puppets Unlimited.* Tara Publishing, 2005. Drawing on a variety of Indian puppet-making traditions, this book encourages children to experiment with materials and ideas to create puppets.